YOUR INNER THERAPIST

YOUR INNER THERAPIST

Eileen Walkenstein, M.D.

UNITY SCHOOL LIBRARY
UNITY VILLAGE, MISSOURI 64065

WITHDRAWN
by Unity Library

bridgebooks
THE WESTMINSTER PRESS
Philadelphia

Copyright © 1983 Eileen Walkenstein

All rights reserved—no part of this book may be repro-
duced in any form without permission in writing from
the publisher, except by a reviewer who wishes to quote
brief passages in connection with a review in magazine
or newspaper.

Book Design by Alice Derr

First edition

Bridgebooks
Published by The Westminster Press®
Philadelphia, Pennsylvania

PRINTED IN THE UNITED STATES OF AMERICA
9 8 7 6 5 4 3 2 1

Library of Congress Cataloging in Publication Data

Walkenstein, Eileen.
  Your inner therapist.

  "Bridgebooks."
  1. Mind and body therapies. 2. Psychology,
Pathological. 3. Medicine, Psychosomatic. I. Title.
RC489.M53W34 1983   616.08   83-19842
ISBN 0-664-26005-5 (pbk.)

To my brother, Bob Walkenstein,
and my friend, Patricia Kind,
who have often been my loving external therapists . . .

And to the ascendance of the Inner Therapist
in everyone

Contents

Introduction 9
Prologue 13

PART I. The Inner Therapist in Physical Garb

Chapter 1. The Shoulders' Hunch—External Physical
                Movement   15
Chapter 2. Controlling the Uncontrollable—
                Internal Physical Movement   23
Chapter 3. Belly Talk—The Ulcerous Rage   37
Chapter 4. Position Is Everything in Life   51
Chapter 5. Messages from Inside   65

PART II. The Inner Therapist in Emotional Garb

Chapter 6. Feeling, Nothing More Than Feeling   77

PART III. Psychological States

Chapter 7. Am I My Neighbor's Keeper?   87

PART IV. Sexual and Relationship Problems

Chapter 8. Love, Where Are Your Eyes?   97

PART V. The Inner Therapist Workbook

Chapter 9. The Inner Therapist Workshop   111

Introduction

The secret life of belly and bone,
Opaque, too near, my private, yet unknown.
—*Delmore Schwartz,*
"The Heavy Bear Who Goes with Me"

Did you ever stop to think that body language isn't merely some expression designed to communicate with others, some show by which others can read you, but is also a way of talking to your self?

Right there in your own body, in its movements, positions, sensations, are messages meant for you. The messages are for your own good. They are repeated in different ways in order to draw your attention to their meaning and to teach you something important about living in general and about your own life in particular.

Mostly we're aware that we do certain obvious things with our bodies, like biting our lips or fiddling with our fingernails, but often the underlying meaning, the deeper lesson meant to help us, escapes. When we don't pay attention to what our body is saying to us, it usually gets more extreme in trying to gain our attention. It becomes like a naughty child who, when the mischievous acts don't work, will throw a tantrum or knock its head on the wall or set fires or swallow poison—anything to get what it needs, a special kind of attending to.

Our body is like that child. When we deprive it of some basic needs, it will act up to remind us that something is wrong, that something needs attending to. On the simplest level, let's say of a deficiency in vitamin C, symptoms of bleeding and ulcerating gums will erupt. Symptoms of scurvy, then, are the body's way of telling us we need vitamin C.

Our body, one way or another, will reveal its needs in a curative attempt to call our attention to those needs. Some studies have

9

shown that when young children don't get enough hugging and touching, that is, when they suffer from a deficiency of contact, they can develop psychosomatic ailments, like asthma, ailments that have been known to clear up on satisfying the needs for contact.

It's clear that within our bodies reside the best teachers for what we need. Conversely, the best way to learn what we need is to learn how to understand their language.

Because these teachers who are built into our systems are there *to serve* our needs, I call them, collectively, the Inner Therapist, from the Greek word meaning "to nurse" or "to serve."

This Inner Therapist resides in every cell of our body as a protective device aimed at keeping us and our species alive and in balance. When we create an imbalance, either by self-destructive or other-destructive acts (as those endangering our species), the Inner Therapist has ways and means to remind us, to wake us up, maybe to punish us if need be in order to get us to change our ways and get into balance again.

What are some of the ways we can learn the language of the Inner Therapist so that we can better learn its lessons and live fuller and better lives? One way, the easiest to study, is through *physical body language*.

Body language is not difficult to read in others. For example, if James greets you with a smile and says how glad he is to see you, but if his hands are tight fists planted firmly into his waist, his arms akimbo, then it's very clear to you (if you're not too much taken in by his smile) that he is challenging you, telling you not to come too close, to keep your distance or else.

Or if Joan says she'd love to hear about your trip to Canada and then, without waiting for your response, rushes on to tell you about her latest experience with her boyfriend, it's clear that she's not really interested in your trip to Canada or any other place, and that at that moment you matter very little except as an audience for her monologue.

We all know how we feel when we reach out a hand expecting to get a good warm and firm handshake only to find the other person's hand feels like a jellyfish, slippery and cool. Ugh!

These examples of others' body language are easy for us to read. We know enough not to expect closeness from a jellyfish unless we turn into one ourselves, or real acceptance from a tightfisted person.

But while most of us are sensitive enough to receive *other* people's signals, we somehow get deaf, dumb, and blind when it comes to receiving our own signals. And we arc capable of harming our *selves* in a destructiveness that no tightfisted, menacing, or phony-smiling pseudo friend can equal. We all know people with precancerous hacking coughs and chest pains who continue to smoke cigarettes. I know a man who had a gangrenous leg amputated as a result of poor circulation who continued to smoke his three packs a day. We all know similar examples—the obese person with diabetes who continues to binge on junk foods, the person with liver damage who continues to booze, and on and on. There is not much harm anyone can do to us that comes near the danger we are to our selves.

On the other hand, the self is capable of helping the self in extraordinary ways. The self can nurse the needs of the self in ways more profound than the ministrations of any other nurse or helpmate, no matter how knowledgeable or well-intentioned. For the self is designed by its very nature to nourish the self, to care for the self, to keep the self in balance.

We have been taught as children to listen to others first and to our *selves* last or not at all. This instruction starts with parents, teachers, other adults, and then all authorities. While some amount of listening to others is of course necessary, when we go too far away from our inner voice we lose our balance, get sick—sick in mind, body, soul, spirit.

What we need in order to become and to remain healthy in mind, body, soul, and spirit, and in all the other aspects of being human, is to regain contact with the Inner Therapist in each of us, to learn how to hear its voice, understand its language, do its bidding.

The Inner Therapist never wishes us harm in any way. It's the good mother, the nourishing earth mother, the warming sun-god and sun-goddess, the fountain of life, the merciful creator, the eternal guide, all wrapped up in one.

The Inner Therapist has one goal—survival. This means survival of ourselves and our species, survival for us and others. That's how we are constructed, that's how we human beings are. Nature provided for us. Nature is not only some force outside, it also resides *inside* each of us. Obviously we can't live without others—we'd never get past infancy on our own. Our individual survival is intimately wrapped up with our species survival. In fact, it is so intimately wrapped up that these—self and species—are one, inseparable, like body and soul.

There are several categories by which the presence of our Inner

11

Therapist makes itself known. One category, the most evident, is *physical*. This can be subdivided into external and internal movement, the external being the easiest to catch hold of.

Another manifestation of the Inner Therapist, also in some instances readily identifiable, is *emotional*. In this category are such feelings as fear, sadness, gloom, anxiety, anger/rage, elation/excitement, and worry.

A third category is *psychological,* which includes such reactions as suspiciousness/distrust/phobia, isolation/loneliness/competitiveness/jealousy, obsessions/addictions, inferiority/superiority.

A fourth category deals with sexual problems, and a fifth with relationship problems. These two categories appear in every one of the first three fundamental categories.

Each category will be described in the succeeding chapters with examples. There will be suggestions about how we can sensitize ourselves, ready ourselves, to receive the messages of that often-disregarded Inner Therapist who speaks to us in many tongues and to whom we owe our health and even our salvation.

Harmony is not just an ideal of the ancient Greeks—it is a requirement of a healthy body and a healthy mind. The task of the Inner Therapist is to keep us in harmonious balance with our selves and with others.

I have undertaken in this book the task of teaching readers the steps they can take to contact their Inner Therapist. The journey may be rocky or precipitous, at times stormy and thunderous—but then, so is nature. Regaining or gaining our contact with our Inner Therapist is like reclaiming our natural heritage.

Prologue

Is this a self-help book?

I'd like to address this question first with a preliminary digression. It's not so much that people desire *self*-help books as that they want to be *led*. The great success recently of so-called self-help books in our nation has come at a time when people are flocking to join cults and to follow leaders.

We want to be told what to do. We don't really want to *help* ourselves as much as we want some *authority* to help us, to take responsibility for us by telling us what's right. In this regard this book is not different from other self-help books. It too has an authority—a psychiatrist—telling readers what to do to achieve harmony in living. But the saving grace of YOUR INNER THERAPIST is that it is truly a guide to that self within the reader, that Inner Therapist who is the ultimate authority for the good life.

Although we *want* to be led by an external authority, what we *need* is to discover and follow our own *internal* authority. Our needs, not our wants, are our lifeline and should therefore be our top priority.

1
The Shoulders' Hunch—
External Physical Movement

The scrimmage of appetite everywhere.
—*Delmore Schwartz*
"The Heavy Bear Who Goes with Me"

By their deeds so shall ye know them.

Yes. And by our deeds so shall we know our selves, and especially that self within, that therapeutic self whose voice we have banished while we fill our ears with our screaming *wants*. When our wants take precedence over our needs we are in trouble, and most of us are in this kind of trouble—unbalanced, topsy-turvy, top-heavy with wantings.

To turn things right side up again we must find a way back to our fundamental *needs*. And we don't have to go very far to do this—no great odyssey, no magnificent hegira. Right there in each of us is an entity who is vitally concerned with the fulfillment of our vital needs. That is its job. *Our* job is to get in touch with that entity.

How to do this?

Do you remember the child's game called "Statues"? In this game a group of children jump or hop around or make grotesque faces until the caller yells out "Freeze!"—whereupon the players are supposed to freeze in the particular position or facial expression they have assumed at that moment.

At this very moment, I'd like to play a variation of that game with you and ask you to suddenly catch any movement of your body by surprise, or any grimace, exactly as it is at this very instant.

Are you jiggling your foot, dilating your nostrils, scratching your head, licking your teeth, clenching your jaw, hunching or bowing your shoulders, frowning, squinting, tightening your fist, spreading your fingers or your toes, holding your breath, breathing shallowly or sighing deeply, contracting your stomach muscles, opening your mouth?

Whatever the motion is, *don't change it!*

That motion that you become aware of is of vital importance to you. It is a subtle indication of an *internal presence.* And it is an opportunity for you to contact that presence.

Don't waste this great opportunity by suddenly acting normal and unhunching—relaxing—your shoulders, if that's what you caught in freeze position. Keep doing it, whatever that "it" is. Exaggerate it a little so that you can be certain it won't go away or that it will be so subtle it will disappear almost at the same instant it reaches your awareness.

Now we are going to play a little theater game with the part or parts that expressed the motion. We are going to make the part the star of the show and give it center stage. It's going to have its own script and speak in its own tongue.

Let's say, for example, that you caught your shoulders tense, hunched up. As soon as you became aware of this, the chances are you felt an immediate tendency to relax them, to drop them down to a normal position (oh, how we want to be normal!).

Whenever we become so obsessed with acting normal and natural, it gets easier to distort ourselves into unnatural shapes and call these natural, while underneath the pseudonatural distortion nature's voice is being stifled, its form warped. Hundreds of thousands of children have been taught (and probably still are), for example, that the "natural" way to breathe is to push out their chests and their shoulders, tighten their stomach muscles and pull in their abdomens. But the exact opposite of this is natural, as any glance at a dog's or an infant's respirations will indicate.

Now, if your shoulders were hunched when I called "Freeze!" and you followed my instructions and allowed yourself to resist your automatic attempt to return to normal once you became aware of their hunchedness, you'll still find them hunched. To exaggerate or caricature the shoulders' deed, hunch them even more, until they feel really tight and uncomfortable. Feel that discomfort. It is not for naught.

Now this is how I might give my own hunched shoulders center stage and their own voice:

First Step: Taking the role of my shoulders, *I describe myself*

16

exactly as I am in the slightly exaggerated state. The monologue might go something like this:

SHOULDERS: I am Eileen's shoulders. I am hunched up, and Eileen's upper arms are under some strain because they have to help keep me up. In my back part, around the neck, I begin to feel a tension. I don't like it. I don't know how long I can keep this up.

Second Step: *I say what I'm doing here, what function my action serves.* I say whatever comes into my mind, no matter how silly or crazy it is. Whatever emerges as I play the role of that part of my body, I let it out. I invent my own dialogue. I, as my shoulders (or other body part), engage in improvisational theater. And nobody's going to boo me off stage.

As with any novice actor, I'm hesitant, don't know what to say, tend to want to *control* what I say instead of *discover* what to say. It's best that I keep at it at first—practice being those shoulders and know that I'll keep going off into control and then on into spontaneity . . . off and on . . . off and on . . . until some flow of conversation finally occurs. And so, my shoulder monologue might run something like this:

SHOULDERS: [I. *Description*]
I'm all hunched up. I don't know how long I can stay this way without getting sore. Why in the world should I hunch up like this? If I keep it up I'll give Eileen a pain in the neck. In fact, that's just what I am—a pain in the neck.

[II. *Function*]
Why am I this way? What function do I serve? H'mmm. Let's see. Well, when I think of what I'm doing, all hunched up like this, I begin to realize that I'm acting as if I'm carrying a heavy weight and I have to keep hunched up in order to support that weight. I guess I'm afraid that if I let myself relax I wouldn't be able to carry the weight.

Ah, so now I know why I need to be hunched—I remind Eileen of the weight she has to carry and that she'd better not relax or the weight will fall off.

Third Step: Once we go this far and get beyond the physical movement description and the function of that movement, we then get into *what that body movement symbolizes.* Body movements, seen as metaphors, are full of messages, and the same movement might symbolize something different for you or you or you, or even something different for me at a different moment in my life. That's why we have to *discover* the monologue, not *decide* what should be said. Once we go this far, then it's time to introduce our customary self—the one we usually think of when we say "I" or the one we think others think of when they address us.

Now center stage has two characters, Hunched Shoulders and Eileen. The two characters improvise a dialogue, each playing her own part. The dialogue might go something like this:

EILEEN: Why do you plague me? You hurt me. I wish you'd relax.
HUNCHED SHOULDERS: I can't relax.
EILEEN: Why not? Why are you so hunched up? You give me a pain.
SHOULDERS: It's *you* who give *me* a pain. You make me carry a heavy weight all the time.
EILEEN: I don't know what you're talking about. What heavy weight? I don't see anything on you.
SHOULDERS: Not a literal weight, dummy. I wouldn't mind that. My muscles are geared to support a physical weight. If I had to carry something from one place to another, I'd do it and get it over with. My job would be done and I'd have a sense of accomplishment. But this weight you put on me is constant. I never get a chance to put it down. Even Atlas got rid of his weight for a time when he turned the world over to Hercules. But you keep me weighted down without even a moment's rest, and I can't stand it. And that's why I retaliate. It's too much of a burden for one set of shoulders to bear.
EILEEN: I don't understand your abstractions. If it's not an actual physical weight, what burden are you talking about?
SHOULDERS: There you go again, putting yet another burden on me. Don't ask me about *your* actions. I've got my own actions to worry about—like hunching myself up when the weight's too heavy. *You* tell *me* what you put on me, then I'll know you really want to carry on a serious conversation.
EILEEN: All right. Don't get so huffy. So I passed the buck. O.K., so you didn't let me get away with it. Let's see. What burdens do I put on you? H'mmm . . . I'm not sure.
SHOULDERS: Well, just now you tried to put the burden on *me* to tell you something that you yourself are responsible for.
EILEEN: So?
SHOULDERS: I'm not going to fall in the trap and answer your questions for you. Answer them yourself.

18

EILEEN: I don't know how.

SHOULDERS: Try.

EILEEN: I can't. I'm blank.

IMPASSE

So here we have an impasse. The dialogue is bogged down, stuck. The two characters are at a standstill, unbudging, but engaged with each other nonetheless, stuck together in frozen combat.

Chances are, if you've followed your own dialogue, you've also come to some sort of impasse. And now, to deal with this dead end, we go to the next step.

Fourth Step: To deal with the impasse effectively, rather than shove it under the rug, where we tend to put all worrisome objects (oh, how we tend to shove everything and everybody that bugs us under that rug and dispose neatly and cleanly of the batch!), we now introduce another character to share the limelight with the other two. On stage comes the Inner Therapist. The spotlight glows with the clarity of the Inner Therapist's vision.

The dialogue continues. Here's one possibility:

EILEEN: Help us! We're stuck.

INNER THERAPIST (that respecter of life, tissue, vital force): That's not bad. You're in good company, Eileen. Those shoulders have been good to you. They've helped you carry packages of food and clothing, two essentials of life. They've enabled your arms to reach out and embrace others, giving you essential contact. They've helped your arms support the weight of carrying your babies and young children and so nurture the succeeding generation. Those shoulders have been very good to you. Not least of all, they have supported your head, obviously an important part of your anatomy. All those functions and considerably more have been the work of your shoulders, work your shoulders were created for. These tasks are wholesome and enhancing. Fine. But you've gone too far.

EILEEN: How?

INNER THERAPIST: Listen to your shoulders and learn. What have they been saying? They complain that the burdens are unwholesome, destructive, that you don't give them any rest. You make them carry more than their share. And then you blame them for hurting and being tense. What would happen if you carried an extra physical weight around with you all the time, let's say even a ten-pound sack? Try it.

19

EILEEN: You mean that literally?

INNER THERAPIST: Yes, of course. It's the only way you'll learn.

EILEEN *(grumbling, reluctantly gets a sack of potatoes and walks around carrying it in her arms. After a few minutes—):* It's beginning to feel heavy. It's beginning to feel like *fifty* pounds! I feel like putting it down.

INNER THERAPIST: See what I mean? And that's only a small sack of potatoes and only a few minutes' worth, and you're already weary. Imagine carrying the heavier weight that your shoulders have to support incessantly, with no respite.

EILEEN *(putting the sack down, relieved to unload the burden):* But what are those weights you're talking about?

INNER THERAPIST: I'll answer that question with a question. What burdens have you been carrying that *do not* belong on your shoulders? We've already talked about your shoulders' rightful work. Now what about work that belongs to other parts of yourself—anatomy or psyche, for example—that you make your poor shoulders assume?

EILEEN: I don't think my shoulders ever do the work of the rest of my body . . . except . . . oh yes, I have a large garage brush whose handle comes loose and the head keeps spinning off when I sweep the driveway. Instead of simply buying a new one, I keep shoving the head back on, hoping to fix it right someday. Sometimes I sweep the leaves, bending over, with only the brush head. So, my shoulders wind up doing more work than they'd need to do if I had a brush that functioned.

INNER THERAPIST: That's a good example on the physical, anatomical level. Now, how do you make your shoulders support the weight of your psyche?

EILEEN: My psyche? You mean my personality?

INNER THERAPIST: All right, your personality.

EILEEN: Uh—well, sometimes I say yes to someone when I really feel like saying no, or I say no to something I want to do when I feel like saying yes. Then I have bad feelings against myself afterward for doing this. The lower I feel about myself, the more I seem to hunch my shoulders.

INNER THERAPIST: Like carrying yourself on your own shoulders? Supporting the weight of that disesteemed self?

EILEEN: Yes, that's it!

INNER THERAPIST: Listen, Eileen. Your shoulders have their own work to do. Their rightful work is very important. You need to respect the work they do for you. When they hunch up, even when you are resting, it's a signal from them to you that they are carrying a burden not their own, an unrightful burden. Hear their plea. You won't be sorry, I promise you. *Don't give them a responsibility that you yourself need to carry.* Struggle with your own yeses and nos—don't make your poor shoulders do that for you.

EILEEN: Yes, I see what you mean. *(Rubbing her shoulders)* Oh, my poor shoulders.

INNER THERAPIST: That's right, make nice. Talk to them.

EILEEN *(to shoulders, no longer hunched):* Dear overburdened shoulders, I'm sorry I've put so much weight on you. You were right to pain me. I give you permission to pain me any time I take undue advantage of you. It'll be a reminder of my copping out on my own responsibilities. Please forgive me. *(Continuing to rub her shoulders)* You feel more relaxed now. I hope I won't take advantage of you again.

SHOULDERS: Don't worry, you will. Old habits die hard. But we'll remind you whenever you slip back. At least you're aware now. Ah, we feel so good when you rub us like that. It makes up for a lot of abuse. Keep it up—we like it.

EILEEN *(smiling):* I feel good when you feel good.

INNER THERAPIST: Yes. It's your job, Eileen, to make your shoulders feel good. And they'll work better for you.

EILEEN: Thanks.

CURTAIN

What are some generalities we can learn from the show we've just seen? Maybe we can best sum it up like this:

1. Each body part has its own natural function.

2. When we place an unnatural demand on a part, it will act up, causing a problem.

3. The problem is not to be *cured.* It needs attending to.

What do we usually do when a body part acts up and causes tension or pain? We reach for a painkiller, a muscle relaxant, a tranquilizer, or a double shot of booze. We seek relief from chemicals. The chemical "relief" creates its own problems. The chemicals make our livers work harder to detoxify them, they make our hearts work harder to push these unnatural substances along the bloodstream, they make our kidneys work harder to eliminate them.

With the "chemical solution" we impose all that extra work on our

21

already imposed upon bodies. And how our bodies groan when we heap these curative burdens on top of the burdensome demands we've already laid upon them!

The body's groan—felt by us as a problem—*needs attention, listening to, not a cure.*

4. When we resist the automatic "reach for a quick cure" and instead give proper attention, this brings us the possibility of hearing the voice of that body part, of listening to its complaints and doing something relevant and constructive.

5. The Inner Therapist is there to show us a way to our natures. It speaks "nature sense" in order to keep us in balance and harmony within our selves and thereby with others. That is its job.

6. Our job is to *discover* that voice of our Inner Therapist, to listen to it, to let it guide us.

2
Controlling the Uncontrollable— Internal Physical Movement

The dance along the artery
The circulation of the lymph
Are figured in the drift of stars.
—*T. S. Eliot,* Burnt Norton

In Chapter 1 we dealt with a common external physical movement of the body, hunching of the shoulders. We could have selected other body movements—nail-biting, scratching, twirling the hair or moustache, pulling at the eyebrows or eyelashes, fingering the nose or the ear, tapping the feet or the fingers, and on and on.

All these external movements can, with little effort, be recognized and brought readily within the control of our wills, at least temporarily. For instance, by a simple decision we can momentarily make our shoulders tense or relax, drum our fingers or keep them still.

The conscious control of any of these movements is easily available to all of us, given sufficient focus and intent. And although it would take some practice for readers to start talking to their shoulders, the hunching or unhunching of those shoulders can readily be performed at will.

The movements so far listed or described are performed by muscles under the control of the central nervous system. All these muscles are called striated muscles, and they are under voluntary control, that is, we can tell them what to do and they will do it.

The nerve pathways of the central nervous system go from the brain down the spinal column and out between the vertebrae to activate the striated muscles of the body. We might even call these muscles "decision" muscles, because we can consciously decide what they should do, how they should move

23

Involuntary movements are under the control of the autonomic nervous system, which is composed of sympathetic and parasympathetic nerve pathways. These nerves go to the smooth muscles, not the striated muscles. Movements of smooth muscles are involuntary, or automatic. We don't have to decide to move them. Their movement takes place even when we're not thinking about them, or about anything. Even when we're in a coma they go on moving inside us.

Until recently in medical history the involuntary movements were thought to be totally automatic, independent, not at all subject to our conscious control. Some of these movements include the dilating or constricting of the pupils of the eyes, constriction or dilatation of the blood vessels (which contain smooth muscles in their walls), and the movement of the gastrointestinal tract. We don't have to decide to breathe or to have our hearts beat the way we decide to pick up a pen and write a letter. Our vital functions are not voluntary, not dependent on our decisions. If they were, there'd be a lot of premature deaths from sheer forgetfulness or absentmindedness. So, especially for those of us who tend to let our minds wander, we're lucky to have some things go on functioning without our having to think about them at all. It's nice not to have to think about everything—there's already too much to think about in this world. And our minds, like complex computer systems, can break down from operation overload. So it's a relief to know that the vital functions—like breathing or heart-beating—don't depend on us.

Well, this automatic out-of-our-control idea was all very good and reassuring, until along came some newer approaches to the body-mind combination that shook up some of these old, comforting ideas. First, some revolutionary type of doctors discovered that the mind does indeed influence the body, and that many physical diseases—such as ulcers, skin eruptions, asthma, anorexia—are actually related to the psyche or the emotions.

The psychosomatic approach promised to take us in a whole new direction, but standing head and shoulders over the young psychosomatic medicine departments and their doctors were the pharmaceutical Goliaths who purveyed drugs for every ailment imaginable and gradually inundated the medical field and the public with increasingly massive advertising campaigns gearing everyone to gobble pills, focus on the soma, and forget the psyche altogether. Even the young and growing psychosomatic departments in hospitals fell prey to the pharmaceutical craze and decided the psyche was far too expensive and difficult to deal with when a pill could kill the pain, stop the attack, alleviate the eruption, tranquilize the mind.

And so, once again, hordes of people voluntarily brought their "involuntary" smooth-muscle disturbances to doctors and pharmacists, who sought to medicate away their symptoms.

Doctors have known all along that the vast majority of their patients (over 70 percent, according to reports in their own medical journals) had nothing wrong with them that a healthier psyche couldn't fix, but they continued to dispense their pharmaceutical notions and potions for the body's alleged ills.

Then, after several decades, another "new" concept emerged: holistic medicine. Once again the entire body was rediscovered—body, mind, soul, spirit, one for all and all for one. And again new departments sprang up, this time in holistic medicine, which dealt with ordinary things that common people could understand, things like proper nutrition (a bastard child previously all but disowned in most medical schools), exercise, avoidance of such poisons as sugars and other simple carbohydrates, avoidance of caffeine, nicotine, chemical additives like artificial colors, artificial flavors, preservatives, and other carcinogenic agents. There were reports alleging that even "incurable" diseases could be cured with nutritional and vitamin approaches. Linus Pauling, Nobel Prize winner, linked vitamin C with cancer cures. Holistic medicine doctors began to report incurable cancer cures with nutritional and psychological approaches.

Whereas three decades ago psychiatrist Wilhelm Reich (author of *Character Analysis, The Function of the Orgasm, The Cancer Biopathy,* etc.) was ridiculed by the medical community for his studies on cancer as a psychosomatic disease—a shrinking of the organism psychologically, energetically, and physically—today one can find in conservative and prestigious medical journals articles on cancer cures related to holistic healing approaches.

Then along came another shot in the arm to the newer approaches. This new shot supported the idea of the power of the mind in dealing with the undealable, the uncontrollable, the smooth muscles that had always been considered beyond voluntary, or conscious, control. Even the smooth muscles in the walls of the independent wild and woolly blood vessels were being corraled in the arena of the psyche, though everyone *knew* that the blood vessels and blood pressure had *nothing* to do with the conscious mind!

25

But the biofeedback approach began to change all of that previous thinking. With a simple, harmless biofeedback apparatus people could lower their own blood pressure! Since hypertension is related to the state of the smooth muscles in the walls of the blood vessels, it was clear that if a way was found to control consciously those usually uncontrollable, independent, autonomous smooth muscles, then we'd have it made—we'd just tell them, order them, to take it easy, to relax, loosen up . . . and presto! our blood pressure would go down.

And that's exactly what happened. Scores of biofeedback centers around the nation began teaching people how to tune in to the state of their blood vessels and to control the uncontrollable.

Something like the following process takes place: First, people with hypertension are taught, often with a little biofeedback device, how to recognize the state of their bodies when their blood pressure is high. With relaxation techniques they are then taught what they have to *do* or *not do* to get the blood pressure lower. When the blood pressure is lower, they begin to recognize what that state *feels* like. And once they learn this, they can presumably bring that state about *at will*. If the treatment is successful, the body ultimately takes over and the person can again relegate the blood pressure to its own control, so to speak.

And so, from biofeedback, nutritional, and holistic approaches (the Pritikin Program, an exercise-nutrition regimen, likewise has claimed marked results in lowering blood pressure) we begin to learn that the smooth-muscle functioning as well as the whole autonomic nervous system can by will or training be made to follow our orders!

One problem I have with these newer advances—let's say the biofeedback approach to lowering blood pressure—is the same problem I have with any symptom approach. We get so wrapped up in curing the symptom that we tend to forget that the symptom arose out of some necessary function it was created to fulfill, and I wonder what more subtle symptom might be created, what subtle assault on the quality of the human life might be perpetrated, under these curative attempts.

I remember the case of a middle-aged man I knew. Clyde was tall, with an average build, bordering on slim. His face had a robust, healthy look. He was in a literature class I attended. I didn't see him for several months owing to a long summer recess. When I saw him again in the fall, he looked awful. His face was drawn and shrunken, and he looked weak. He told me valiantly that he had been on the Pritikin Program and that he had lost weight and his blood pressure had dropped 40 points since starting the program. He said he felt victorious and smiled a wan smile. His facial expression was strained. I couldn't get the image of that drawn, shrunken visage with its forced smile out of my mind. It seemed that the smile was an effort, a pleasureless grimace. The fat was literally gone out of his life and his expression, as it was gone out of his diet. In fact, he had a cancerous look. But undeniably his blood pressure was lower.

The biofeedback and Pritikin approaches are certainly great advances in encouraging the individual's coping mechanism, and giant steps away from the pharmaceutical-dependency morass that our culture has sunk into. But I'd hate to think that the body went to all that trouble to develop a symptom and that we blithely found a way to combat the body's own creation by curing its symptom, with such indifference to its cause.

Every psychosomatic symptom, including the most noxious from high blood pressure to bleeding ulcers, is created out of some functional need. I hate to think of combating the body's creation without learning what that creation, that symptom, is trying to teach us and what underlying need forged the symptom in the first place. If there's a lesson to be learned from the symptom that will deepen our life's experience, fill out our squashed-in places, flesh out our shrunken spirits, then to cure the symptom, which contains the voice of our teacher about life, is paradoxically to combat life itself.

The biofeedback approach is important as a first step because it gives us a contact with the symptom, an awareness of what is. If we have high blood pressure, biofeedback helps us tune in to the state of our blood vessels and their musculature. Fine and good. The first necessary step is *awareness*. And the biofeedback certainly trains us to focus our awareness.

But then we have to take another step. For if we stay only with the physical awareness of the symptom and learn nothing of the human function it serves—what it means in psychological and emotional and relationship terms, and why it was created in the first place—we have added nothing to the deeper quality and understanding of the person's life and have merely mechanized the robot to act more efficiently.

What *is* the next step?

Recall in the first chapter the steps to resolving the problem with the hunched shoulders? The first step taken was to describe the actual physical state of those shoulders. In the case of the voluntary muscles, this is not too difficult to achieve—after all, we can touch them, look at them, decide to move them, and see their movement. They are out in the open—clearly visible. But this is not so with our smooth muscles, which are hidden away inside the sealed envelope of our skins. To complicate our learning about what's on the inside of our body, the majority of us, and especially women, have historically been deprived of learning even about the body's *outside*. Many women still think they have only two openings in their private regions, even after childbirth experience. We'll go further toward illuminating this dark subject in a later chapter when we talk about sexual functioning.

Now, describing the actual physical state of those out-of-sight muscles takes being educated as to what they look and act like there under the covers of our skin. Describing them is the first step, as we noted, toward the awareness of what is, and this requires some instruction about healthy and sick body tissues.

To start with the heart of the matter, we can begin with the pipeline from the heart—namely, the blood vessels with their smooth-muscle walls. The blood-vessel system is an elastic pipeline through whose walls selectively pass oxygen and other substances to nurture the surrounding tissues. Because certain substances permeate, or seep through, the rubbery walls, while certain other substances are kept inside, the quality of the walls of the blood vessels in the natural healthy state is said to be semipermeable or selectively permeable.

Our blood pressure depends in part on the condition of the walls of the small peripheral blood vessels (as opposed to the larger central vessels). All blood-vessel walls, in the healthy state, are elastic, flexible, yielding (to greater or lesser quantities of blood), and semipermeable (letting things come in and go out). I suppose we'd be happy to be around people whose personalities have a nice balance of these qualities too. And we'd be lucky if these people happened to be our parents—what a good start in life that would be!

The pumping action of the heart, which pushes the contents of the blood vessels along, is helped by the elasticity of the vessel walls. One could say that the more elastic the blood vessels are, the easier the work of the heart is. Elasticity is essential for proper functioning—elasticity, stretchability, pliability, and semipermeability. If all these qualities are present, the chances are our blood pressure would be normal and our hearts grateful.

28

On the other hand, when the smooth muscles in the blood-vessel walls are contracted, stiff, rigid, unyielding, or hardened (calcified), they lose their rubber-band resiliency and threaten the heart by increasing its work load. Overworked hearts have to get bigger and bigger to continue to carry their increasing load—a condition known as hypertrophy, that is, super-growth. While this is all right for biceps, as any weight lifter will attest, it's not so good for the moaning heart.

To complicate the problem further, these rigidifying changes in the walls of the blood vessels cause a slowing of the blood flow— stasis. "Stasis" means standing still. When the blood "stands still" long enough, plaques are likely to form on the inner surface of the vessel walls. Plaques are dangerous because they are easy resting places for blood clots to form on. When the clot gets so big that it fills the entire opening (lumen) inside the blood vessel, there is a sudden cutoff of circulation, and the tissues normally supplied by that vessel begin to die (necrosis). If this happens in blood vessels in brain tissue, we might suffer a sudden stroke; if it happens in the vessels of the heart (coronary arteries), we might get a heart attack.

All of this explanation is a small attempt to help those who are fuzzy about these vascular details. I hope this little knowledge will not prove to be a dangerous thing but will form a base for understanding what's going on inside us. Our Inner Therapist "knows" all this, but *we* need some educating to know how to tune in to what our Inner Therapist knows so we can allow ourselves to be guided to a fuller and better-functioning life.

Keeping in mind the first scene from Chapter 1 (featuring the hunched shoulders) and keeping in mind the description of nonelastic, constricted, and rigid blood vessels, you should be able to follow this next scene and perhaps use it as a guide to construct one for yourself out of your own inventiveness.

Let us consider George, a fifty-five-year-old businessman, hypertensive and power-driven. His blood vessels are tight and his blood pressure, like his corporate worth, is always on the rise. And, first things first, let us hear from his blood vessels, the peripheral ones. They have center stage.

SCENE I

GEORGE'S (PERIPHERAL) BLOOD VESSELS *(and the muscles in their walls):* We are constricted most of the time. We do very little relaxing. We are tense, tight, nonyielding, becoming more and more rigid. Because of our condition, our decreased elasticity, we cause the pressure of the blood flowing through us to rise. Another result of our decreased elasticity is that we inhibit the blood flowing through us so that it flows more sluggishly. Sometimes, because the flow is sluggish, it slows down so much that it helps create plaques on our inner walls, and blood forms a clot there. The slower the blood flows, the bigger the clot grows. If the clot grows big enough, it'll plug up our insides and stop the blood flow altogether. Since none of George's body parts can live without blood flowing to them, bringing life-necessary oxygen to their cells, when the blood supply is cut off, the parts begin to die.

So you see how powerful we are. We have the power to control George's pressure and blood flow. You might say we hold George's life in our walls. The more relaxed and elastic we are, the more life we allow to flow into George's tissues. You might also say we are his lifeline. Certainly we are his blood-line.

Conversely, the more constricted we are, the more rigid we are, the more death we deal out.

SCENE II

Enter GEORGE

GEORGE: Why do you plague me? You know how uptight I get every time I go to my doctor and she tells me my blood pressure is up another 20 points. Then she has to increase my medication to combat my blood pressure, and the medication wreaks havoc with my potency. You're destroying my sex life.

Why can't you just relax so I can get on with my life? Can't you see how much I have to do? I have orders to fill, employees to handle, business meetings to arrange and conduct, travel schedules to keep, time limits, time pressures, time demands, time exigencies. Why don't you just get more yielding and let my blood flow easier so I don't have to have this pounding in my heart every time my blood pressure rises?

BLOOD VESSELS: Ha ha! Oh, that's a good one!

GEORGE: You think it's funny that I have this pounding in my ears, these cramps in my legs at night, that I have to listen to my doctor's warnings about how high my pressure is getting and be told about the dire consequences? I don't see anything funny in my life. You're out of sync!

BLOOD VESSELS *(still chuckling):* Look who's calling *us* out of sync!

Listen, man, you've been out of sync with us for years. When did you ever beat to our rhythm? Do you think we just up and rigidified over night? Just all at once with a snap of your fingers? We're not like your employees, you know, who have to put up with your excessive demands, who give up their lunch hours and vacations for any last-minute whim of yours. No, we have a life of our own, and when the going gets rough for us we know how to slow down. You can't drive us like you do your employees or your business deals. We know how to resist you, and resist you we will.

GEORGE: I don't have time to hang around trying to cajole you. I have too much to do. I'll just get my doctor to increase my medication so I can go on. I'll control you yet.

BLOOD VESSELS: If you think the way to control us is to dictate your terms to us, you've got another think coming. We'll just dig in more, tighten up more. The more you fight us, the more unyielding we'll become. You won't get any elasticity from us.

GEORGE: I won't put up with these threats. I refuse to go on with this discourse.

BLOOD VESSELS: Fine. At least we won't have to listen to your blabber.

IMPASSE

SCENE III
Enter George's INNER THERAPIST

INNER THERAPIST: What's going on here? There's some kind of impasse. That's what summoned me. How can I help?

(GEORGE *and* BLOOD VESSELS *speak at once*)

GEORGE: My blood vessels are insufferable!
BLOOD VESSELS: George is giving us a hard time. He's impossible!

INNER THERAPIST: Wait a minute. One at a time, please. George, since you never wait for anybody or anything, it might be good practice for you to wait your turn. Go last for a change.

GEORGE: But—

INNER THERAPIST: Now, just slow down and listen for a change. Just because you're listening doesn't mean you have to buy it. Just close your mouth and open your ears.

GEORGE *(grumbling):* All right, all right.

INNER THERAPIST: Now, Blood Vessels, what's your view of the problem?

BLOOD VESSELS: Once we were resilient like a bouncing rubber ball,

31

stretching up and down, out and in, as the blood coursed through us—elastic. That's when George was younger and treated us better.

Then he entered the corporate world and began abusing us. He boozed and ate plenty at those business meals, polluting our bloodstream and making us grow extra miles of blood-vessel tracks through the excess tonnage he created. He kept running here and there and everywhere, never getting enough sleep for us to rest up and bounce back again. He kept filling our insides with too much fatty meats and rich sugar foods, which caused plaques inside our walls.

But then he began pressuring us. The more tense he became over some business deal, the more he'd pressure us, until we had no choice but to try to resist all that pressuring.

So—you know the story. First we resisted by tensing up and contracting, especially the smallest ones among us, the peripheral ones. The longer George stayed pressuring us, the longer we stayed contracted, until we caused George's blood pressure to shoot up so high he had to take notice, and so did his doctor. Then, the longer we stayed contracted, the stiffer we became. But the stiffer the burdens George assumed, and the more he pushed his business deals through against huge odds, the stiffer the burdens he placed on us, until we began to get not only stiff but rigid. We began to lose our natural elasticity. And of course, George's B.P. really went haywire after that.

GEORGE: Hey, wait a minute. Hold it! Are you saying that I caused you to get rigid, that I created my own high B.P.?

INNER THERAPIST: Don't get so excited, George. Just think of the positive aspects. If you created your own high blood pressure, then you can uncreate it. If you cause your high blood pressure because of your way of life and your attitude toward your business practices, then you can cause it to get lower too—just by a change in the way you conduct your life and your work and your relationships. Don't balk at it—just think of the power you have to change things.

GEORGE: But I've always worked under pressure. I get more done in a day than most people do in a week. That's how I've always been. You can't expect me to change all that. Besides, my work demands that I don't change.

INNER THERAPIST: And your body demands that you do. You've put your work above your body, your business success above your life. As a result, your body and its life suffer. You've got your priorities upside down. You drive your body, pressure it, abuse it, in order to achieve nonbody goals. I might say you sacrifice your body, your blood vessels, for the Goddess Success. Your type of business success, by its very nature, causes your body's failure.

GEORGE: I don't get it. Why can't I have a healthy business *and* a healthy body? You sound as though I can't have both.

INNER THERAPIST: It's apparent that you don't have both. That is your reality. I don't deal with what might be if. I deal with present realities. And your present reality is that you're a smashing success in the eyes of the business world, while you smash your body and make it groan under the pressures and abuses you heap on it. And your poor blood vessels are turning into railroad tracks to keep your steam engine speeding along at a breakneck pace!

GEORGE: Yes, but I can't slow down. Too much depends on me.

INNER THERAPIST: If you keep up your frenzied drive toward success, you'll soon be the most successful corpse in the cemetery.

GEORGE: Uh . . . yeah. That's what my doctor's been telling me.

INNER THERAPIST: Is that where you're driving to?

GEORGE: Well, no. I don't want that. I don't want to die. But I don't know any other way to live.

INNER THERAPIST: Are you willing to learn another way?

GEORGE: Well, uh, yes. Yes. I've got to. I can't stand these pressures in my head any more. Sometimes it feels like the top of my head is going to blow right off. All right. I do want to change, if it's possible. Anything to get rid of these pressures in my head.

INNER THERAPIST: George, first you must realize that I, as your Inner Therapist, am interested in only one thing—your survival. You must realize that business matters, or the view the world has of you, or fame and power and all that jazz, are irrelevant to me. The survival of yourself and your species— your personal survival and how you contribute to the survival of others—this survival business is paramount and my ultimate concern.

GEORGE: Yes, I know that my survival is your business.

INNER THERAPIST: And it's *your* business to know what's going on in your body. Now, in the case of your blood vessels, they've been trying to tell you something you need to listen to. When they

33

say their smooth muscles in their walls are tense, how does this characteristic relate to you?

GEORGE: Well, *I'm* tense most of the time.

INNER THERAPIST: Exactly. Now, to study *your* tension is *your* job.

GEORGE: How do I do that?

INNER THERAPIST: First, get yourself a large notebook. It's a worthwhile investment, probably one of the best investments you'll ever make.

GEORGE *(objecting):* Wait a minute, there. I hope you don't expect me to write anything in it. I just can't afford that kind of time.

INNER THERAPIST: George, you can't afford not to. I told you, this will be the best investment you've ever made.

GEORGE *(grumbling):* All right, all right. What am I supposed to do?

INNER THERAPIST: I want you to start by writing a list of all the people and things in your life right now that make you tense. When you've finished that list, make a second list of everything and everyone that makes you feel relaxed or less tense. This will be a tiny list at this time, in contrast to the first list, but never mind that. Your willingness to write these lists and start focusing your attention on these items is like giving yourself a biofeedback exercise. The *attention* itself increases your *awareness* and increases your contact with the state of tensions in your body, including the tensions in the muscles of the walls of your blood vessels.

A further problem your blood vessels complain of is that they are becoming stiff, unbending, inelastic, unyielding, rigid, and pressured. Now, what do *these* qualities suggest to you, what do they remind you of?

GEORGE *(reluctantly):* Well, I've been accused of being rigid and unbending, not only in business deals but also in my demands on my employees and even in my family.

INNER THERAPIST: Yes, and pressured too.

GEORGE: I admit that. But as I said before, this is an old pattern of mine and I can't help being this way.

INNER THERAPIST: Yes you can. Don't you see that your blood vessels are expressing and becoming precisely what you are doing in your life and how you are in your life?

GEORGE: But how can I change all that?

INNER THERAPIST: By taking the next necessary step toward awareness. You can start right now with Step Two. In your notebook write a description of all your activities in which you are stiff,

34

rigid, unyielding, and pressured. Don't omit any—from your business to your sex life to your relationship with your children and their demands, etc. Be as specific and detailed as possible. Look at it all as through a magnifying glass, and write it all down. It's important that you make sure to do this writing when you are alone and without a time limit and without any surrounding distractions.

Another important item—decide in advance that you're not going to show the notebook to anyone. Thus you don't have to censor anything. The notebook is just for you, me, and your body. It's nobody else's business. In fact, if you let someone else in on it, *their* reactions will influence what you subsequently write in *your* notebook, and we don't want anyone else in it. This is your own direct line to yourself, to be responded to by no one but yourself.

Your notebook is your biofeedback apparatus to awaken your consciousness to your own body's functioning.

GEORGE: I'm beginning to understand.

INNER THERAPIST: You will learn, George, that the body is *designed* to help itself, to keep itself in balance, to grow and mature. It's the very nature of the body to take care of itself. It's your job to let your body do its task and not interfere.

GEORGE: How do I do that?

INNER THERAPIST: Back to the notebook. After you've described every way you've been too rigid, demanding, pushy—the where, with whom, when, how, what—you are ready for the next step.

You are to keep a daily log of every incident in which these pushy characteristics show up. Again, the log must be written when you have some privacy and no time limit. It needs to be given priority time. It needs to be your top priority, because if you don't solve this problem, you simply won't survive to satisfy any other priority.

GEORGE: I don't like taking the time for this, but I'm willing to give it a try.

INNER THERAPIST: Good. You don't have to like it. Remember, we're concerned here not with your *likes* but with your *needs*. You need to do this.

GEORGE: But will writing all this down really lower my blood pressure?

INNER THERAPIST: It's an essential step toward lowering your blood pressure. What's needed is your awareness of your pressured and pressuring life in exact, excruciating detail, with a daily accounting and a full set of minutes—that will wake you up to your reality.

GEORGE: Agreed!

BLOOD VESSELS *(having been silent and patient all this time):* We're already beginning to feel relieved!

CURTAIN

Everything we do in our lives is reflected in our body, seeps into every cell of our tissues and wields its influence.

George's story is more extreme than most. We don't all wheel and deal in the stratosphere of the corporate world of high finance. But there are innumerable men and women in more modest jobs who are pressured by the demands of their individual time, or pressured by and pressure their families. There are many who experience, in their own less flamboyant but equally pressured ways, what George experienced in his way. No matter what your status, your way and manner of life dominates every cell in your body.

If we read the body's symptoms as metaphors, messages, that can teach us something about the way we are living our lives, then there is something we can learn in order *to eradicate not the symptom but the need for it.* After all, the symptom is there to wake us up to the presence of an imbalance. It cries out to us to correct the imbalance. We shouldn't want to kill the town crier. We should want to correct the source of the disastrous news.

Is that notebook really all that it takes? Is it really effective as a biofeedback device? Will it really lower your blood pressure and relax your blood vessel muscles?

Is it worth a try? Is your body worth the sacrifice of your time and investment in the notebook? Ask your own Inner Therapist for the answers.

And remember, awakening to the awareness of what is is the dawning of change. Have a good new day!

3
Belly Talk—
The Ulcerous Rage

Why does he smile and bow to me so low
When he mentions that my foot is fairly heavy on his toe,
Or beg my pardon with such grace
When I have shoved him from his place?
                    —*Author, "The Apologist"*

It will but skin and film the ulcerous place,
Whilst rank corruption, mining all within,
Infects unseen.
—*Shakespeare,* Hamlet, *Act 3, Scene 4*

Did you ever watch a baby's face after nursing, after the baby has been cuddled and comforted? Have you noticed how relaxed it is, how it glows? Have you felt how warm it is, thanks to the flowing blood supply?

That picture of the baby's face is similar to the inside of your stomach when *you* are relaxed, cuddled, and comforted.

The normal stomach lining is pink; its juices flow moderately. Its walls are relaxed and moving with a gentle peristaltic movement, as does the rest of the gastrointestinal tract. There's just enough hydrochloric acid produced by the cells to aid the stomach in its job of digestion.

When you treat your stomach with tender care, it too will respond to your attentions with a pink glow.

What happens when the same baby cries for food or comfort and nobody pays attention? It begins to thrash around, to cry louder. Look at its face—it begins to contort with frustration and then with rage. Its neck veins stand out, the facial muscles contract as the baby starts howling. After a while the teary eyes become bloodshot, the face becomes beet red—rage red. In fact, the entire body contracts as in spasm.

If you've followed the analogy, you can probably guess the stomach's plight when *it* is enraged. Yes, it actually becomes red, an angry red. It contracts, and the tears of frustration are not salt but acid—copious, burning, acid tears. This is a description of the stomach of an ulcer sufferer. What was thrashing in the baby becomes hypermotility in the stomach. One might say the stomach is thrashing around in its way just as the baby was thrashing in its way. Gone is the gentle peristaltic undulating movement—the gentle wave has become a cyclone, an ocean in an uproar.

The torrents of pouring-out juices produce hyperacidity, a burning red-hot fiery production. The walls of the stomach are red—raging red—and contracted.

When all that hypermotion, with its super-acid torrents and contractions, goes on for a time, the normally smooth lining of the stomach or duodenum (the long, narrow small intestine leading from the stomach) becomes rough from all the harsh treatment, and after a time, not being able to maintain its smooth interior conditions, it may have a blowout—a hole in its lining. This hole is called an ulcer. That's what an ulcer is: a hole, an open sore. If the hole gets deep enough, it begins to bleed.

While all that conflagration is happening inside, what's happening outside with the person whose stomach it is?

Believe it or not, sometimes the person doesn't even *know* what's happening while this internal eruption is taking place. Sometimes a peaceful exterior state exists with no obvious symptoms. This is called a silent ulcer, and the person may not discover its existence until the feces turn black (from blood leaking into the intestines, the iron in the hemoglobin turning the stool black). These people are not so lucky as you'd imagine, because silent ulcers of the stomach may develop into stomach cancers.

Most ulcers, however, appear in the walls of the small intestine at the upper part of the duodenum. They are therefore called duodenal ulcers and are usually very painful.

What else may be happening on the outside while all that tumult is going on internally? Aside from reaction to the pain of the ulcer, nothing.

And that's just the point. The typical ulcer type of person keeps

38

everything in. Nothing much shows on the outside, especially rage. The stored-up, heaped-up, hoarded-up, pushed-down-inside rage has to go somewhere to keep the person in some sort of balance, so it breaks out on the inside. It's as if the ulcer type, with the earliest inkling of angry feelings, immediately banishes these forbidden reactions to the prison walls of the gut, while the face and personality adopt a smooth, calm, aim-to-please demeanor. The more venom the person swallows, the more acquiescent the exterior show, the more the outraged stomach or intestine has to bear the brunt. So it expresses its fury by setting up a tantrum inside. It bursts the walls and develops a sore (an ulcer, a hole, a blowout) to show how *sore* it is—all this to balance the excessive calm on the exterior.

Do you have an ulcer? Do you know what I mean? If you don't believe your insides are enraged while you are becalmed, ask yourself what you felt like, in your abdomen, when someone put you down or got you upset, especially if that someone was an authority person.

I'd better digress to say what I mean by "authority person." It's not just a boss or supervisor who has power over you and can hire or fire you at will. No, nothing so obvious. And it's not just a policeman who can haul you in for suspicious behavior.

The "authority" is often more subtle. It can be anyone you elevate to a position of judging you—anyone whose approval you're anxious to have. It can be a gas station attendant or a bus driver or someone else in uniform—the uniform itself evokes an authority of sorts. It can be your spouse or your child, and certainly a parent. Anyone to whom you delegate the power and the right to tell you that what you're doing is terrible or great, good or bad—whose good graces you may seek—is your "authority."

It can even be a snotty kid lurching along the sidewalk as you walk by, or a "corner bum" outside the local hangout. When you let any snicker or remark from them get to you, that makes them your instant authority.

I knew an overweight woman whose entire day was ruined when she overheard a five-year-old in a department store say to her mother, "Look at that fat lady, Mommy!" The innocent five-year-old became the forty-year-old fat woman's instant judgmental and critical authority, ruling over her feelings for the rest of the day and into the night.

Back to *you,* if you are an ulcer type. Did you stand up for yourself

39

when some recent authority put you down? Did you dare to answer back, voice your disagreement if not your anger—or did you merely smile civilly, nurse your anger in silence, and store it inside so efficiently that you didn't even know it was there?

Here we have a situation similar to those of the shoulders and the blood vessels in the preceding chapters. When we don't do what's called for, when *we* don't take responsibility for our responses, our body has to do it for us. In this way we put an unnatural burden on the body, for whenever we are angry and don't deal with it, when we push it inside so we no longer know it's there, *our insides do what we have shirked*. They carry our burden for us. They pay the cost of our shirking.

If you are overly sensitive to all the authorities around you, there's one thing you can be grateful for—at least you're responsive. You're not a zombie or a robot. You're still connected to the human race, even if that connection is painful and demeaning and destroying your insides. It's hoped you'll be able to do something about the pain of it all with the help of your Inner Therapist, especially if you learn what all those present authorities are substitutes for. That is, who is the *real* authority you have spent your life trying to please?

The crazy thing about our computer-like brains is that they are storage bins (maybe garbage cans too) of everything that's been thrust into us. Especially invulnerable to riddance are the earliest things in our lives—and the earliest people. I've seen adults drive themselves crazy still trying to please a parent who had been dead for years. Of course, the earliest and most important authority in our lives is the person who most parented us, on whom we depended for our very breath. And often pleasing her or him was an actual matter of life or death.

With the former discussion as a program note, we are in a position to understand the "belly talk" and are now ready for the curtain to rise on "Hot to Trot on the Ulcer Trail."

We will select as the star of the show someone at random from the masses of ulcer sufferers. It might be any one of you out there. Let's choose Steve, a thirty-two-year-old elementary school teacher. Keeping in mind the importance of the earliest influences, we have to mention Steve's father, a robust, successful businessman. Steve's father came from a long line of spare-the-rod-and-spoil-the-child types who passed on the concept to each succeeding generation along with the whippings with those unspared rods in their various evolutionary forms (switches, rods, cat-o'-nine-tails, rulers, belts, etc.).

Most of Steve's male forebears went into the family business. Steve was the first major departure. His father was not too upset, because Steve's older brother, whom his father clearly favored, did the family thing and joined the family business, bringing to it a prestigious business college degree.

Steve had a strange fear which he barely voiced to anyone, namely, that if he ever succeeded too well, his father wouldn't like him, might even get angry with him. This underlying competitive fear of his father was more a feeling than a clear thought. (I've seen this same fear in many sons of driving, success-oriented business-men.) For Steve, becoming a teacher was like withdrawing from the competition and letting his father and older brother win.

Once in a while his father made jokes about Steve's profession—something about only girls and sissies becoming teachers. Steve swallowed those gibes along with all the other put-downs, but they hurt more than the belt-lashings his father used to give him. The physical beatings became rare after Steve early dedicated himself to pleasing his father.

The peculiar thing, though, was that his father seemed paradoxi-cally *displeased* with Steve's attempts to please him. The more Steve tried, the more rejecting his father seemed to be.

Steve had vowed he would be gentle and accepting with his own children, but his two sons turned out to be wild, destructive, often hostile, as if to prove how right his father had been in never sparing the rod. And it seemed a foregone conclusion that when they grew up they would be the type of father to use the rod with *their* children, spittin' images of their grandfather.

To top it all off, guess what kind of woman Steve married — someone just like his father! Why did he go and do a thing like that? Why do so many people marry persons who turn out to have the worst aspects of the parent who gave them the most difficulty?

I believe that people do this, not to torment themselves or to wallow in masochism, but to reproduce an earlier conflict and thus give themselves an *opportunity to resolve it* and grow beyond it. This is another example of Nature's trying to correct itself, improve itself, reach perfection. Even a rat will bite off its own leg to get out of a trap and save its life. In all of life there's some surge toward survival, growth, and maturity, the "force that through the green fuse drives the flower."

41

We all have this force. To become whole and ripened into adulthood we have to unhook ourselves from the stages and the conflicts where we have remained stuck in the past. We all need to grow beyond the diaper stage, so to speak. And somehow or other we and our bodies keep trying to get into those stuck areas, not to revel in the pain, but in order to unhook and grow from there. This, I believe, is a basic law which pervades all life forms.

Back to Steve, who aimed to please his not-to-be-satisfied father, his likewise wife, and his disorderly sons. They all became his authority figures, while he sought their never forthcoming approval.

And what was it like for Steve at his job in a big-city public school? More authority figures—an entire classroom of them—in addition to the principal and the superintendent! All those authorities to bow before, while his stomach contracted more and more.

Finally Steve is readying himself to face his belly.

HOT TO TROT ON THE ULCER TRAIL

SCENE I

Enter STEVE *and his* BELLY

STEVE: You hurt so much. Sometimes I have to double over with the pain. And when I'm upset about something, you come on especially strong. It's bad enough when I'm already bothered— like when the principal calls me in for some parent's complaint—but then you add to it with your gnawing pains, and it becomes just about intolerable.

BELLY: You've got it all backward. It's *you* who hurts me. I like to be calm and smooth—that's my natural state. But you always get me in an uproar.

STEVE: I don't know what you're talking about. I don't see how I can create an upheaval for you. People are always telling me I'm one of the calmest guys they know.

BELLY: Exactly. You are calm at *my* expense. Instead of your giving out with a roar, *I* have to rear up and do the roaring for you.

STEVE: But I don't know how to roar. That's for wild beasts, not for civilized human beings. The world would be a terrible place if every human being started screaming and yelling.

BELLY: Wrong again. You have vocal cords that allow for yells as well as whispers. You're always at the whisper end of the spectrum, so I have to do your yelling for you to keep you in balance. And do I yell! Judging from the furious red color of my walls, my wild contractions, my energetic flow of acid—judging from *my* display, *you* must have an awful lot of raging you're pushing down into me. You sure are a pushy guy!

STEVE: I've never been accused of being pushy.

BELLY: No, of course not. I'm the one you push.

STEVE: It can't be. I'm simply not aggressive. I believe in cooperation, not competition. I have no rage.

BELLY: No, *I* have it all, and in spades, because you won't take on the job. It's not my natural job. I was put in this world to store and deal with your food, not your rage.

STEVE: I still haven't the foggiest notion what you're driving at.

BELLY: Aw, shut up already!

IMPASSE

SCENE II

Enter Steve's INNER THERAPIST *to the rescue*

INNER THERAPIST: Ah, the impasse—like a knell that summons me. It seems you don't understand one another.

BELLY: You're darned right we don't!

INNER THERAPIST: Why are you so belligerent?

BELLY: You would be too if someone made you do his dirty work for him, especially if you weren't equipped to do it.

STEVE: I don't know what dirty work he's referring to.

INNER THERAPIST: Just a minute, both of you, or we'll be going in circles again, as you've both been doing for years with such disastrous results. I'd like you each to state your case, one at a time.

BELLY: I'll go first. And that's just the point. *I* have to lead because Steve never does. He pulls back from every confrontation, and that leaves *me* needing to take the lead. When I lead—that is, when Steve leads with his gut instead of his personality—I hurt him, because it's unnatural for me to have to lead. It's not my job, and I'm not equipped to handle it without damaging myself and hurting him in the process. And when I hurt him, he complains, gets more upset, runs to doctors for medicines, ulcer diets . . . and he keeps worrying about blood loss and anemia when my load gets too heavy and I develop a blowout.

INNER THERAPIST: Steve, what have you to say?

STEVE: I do suffer terribly from gnawing pains. I have to watch what

43

and when I eat. Sometimes it's unbearable, but I try never to take sick leave from work. As a result, I'm often in pain while I'm trying to teach. And the children in my class are admittedly unruly very often, and I can't seem to calm them down any more than I can calm down my gut.

INNER THERAPIST: When else are you in a situation where you have trouble getting things calmed down?

STEVE: Well, at home my sons are unruly too. They want their own way all the time, even when it's not good for them—like watching TV instead of doing their homework or reading a book. And they never get enough sleep because they stay up so late watching their TV shows. Then I can't get them up in the mornings. Every morning it's a problem trying to get them to school on time, and often we all have to miss breakfast so as not to be late.

INNER THERAPIST: Where is your wife in all this conflict?

STEVE: Well, to tell the truth, I try to keep her out of it because she flies off the handle so easily. And there's no stopping her once she gets going. She used to hit them, which was very painful for me. So I've taken on the task of waking the boys and getting them breakfast and off to school in the morning. And in the evenings the boys get rambunctious, fight, throw things at each other. We have rarely ever had a peaceful meal or a calm evening. But often my wife goes out to meetings at night, and then at least I don't have to get in a conflict with her.

INNER THERAPIST: What kind of conflict?

STEVE: She doesn't seem to be satisfied with anything I do. There's always some kind of criticism. I try to be understanding—I know the boys aren't an easy job—but she blames everything on me.

BELLY: Yeah, that's just when he puts the burdens on me.

INNER THERAPIST: Yes, we're getting to that. Steve, do you understand what your belly has just said?

STEVE: I don't understand how *I* would willingly put the burden on my own stomach. But it is true that after a hassle my stomach does feel knotted up.

INNER THERAPIST: Yes, that's what your belly has been trying to tell you. There's a direct tie-in between the fights and your stomach tensions.

STEVE: But how can I help that? The hassles seem so inevitable.

44

INNER THERAPIST: They *are* inevitable under the present circumstances. But *people can change circumstances.*

STEVE: How? I've been trying for years to change things.

INNER THERAPIST: That's just it. You've been trying and trying, and always doing the same old things. Trying is never enough. You could try to get off a chair and walk across the room for some food, but as long as you remain in the chair trying, without getting up and going across the room—that is, as long as you keep trying instead of doing—you could starve to death. You've been trying to change while you keep placating everyone, seeking everyone's approval. That has been your major problem and the major problem of your stomach.

BELLY: Yeah, he was so busy getting their approval, he never thought of me, of getting my approval. All along it was my approval he should have been looking for. He put everyone above me and never paid attention till it was too late and I burst out in a bleeding ulcer. And even then what does he do? He still doesn't pay the proper attention. He drags himself to doctors and tries to quiet me down with medicines of different sorts, and doesn't give me the *attention* I need!

STEVE: It's true I went to doctors and got prescriptions. I didn't know what else to do.

INNER THERAPIST: Yes, you did what most people do in our "pill age." You took the easy way out.

BELLY: And wreaked pillage on me!

INNER THERAPIST: You took the medicine, Steve, and followed the authority of the doctors, instead of doing the difficult task of struggling to exert your own authority and asking yourself what the painful symptoms were doing there in the first place. Nor did you face the even more painful truth hiding within the symptom. You sought a solution instead of an understanding, which would have brought with it many solutions. And so you quieted your ulcer from time to time, but did nothing to solve your larger problem, which your belly's symptoms were trying to alert you to.

STEVE: I did *feel* the symptoms, though. They were frequently so painful I couldn't help feeling them. The pain often awakened me at night.

INNER THERAPIST: Yes, you felt your belly's pain, but you didn't hear its voice, its messages. You were awakened from your sleep but never *to* your life.

45

STEVE: Yes, I suppose if I were to face the truth I'd have to admit my *life* is painful, my *relationships* are troublesome—at home, at work, everywhere.

INNER THERAPIST: Precisely. That's why you buried the pain of your relationships in the first place—it was too hard to take. When you were a helpless child you may have had no choice but to submit, to bury the pain of your father's excessive demands, of his never approving of you, of his incessant criticism. But now you're grown, you have your own feet to stand on, your life doesn't depend on your parents' approval any longer. You don't keel over if they—or any of the *theys* out there—disapprove of you. You may not like it—no one likes disapproval—but you will not die from it, as you feared you might when you were a child dependent on an enraged father. At that time, to get some semblance of nurturing from your rejecting father, you had to subserve him, please him. A smile or a hug is a necessary stroke for an infant. It's as much an urgency as milk itself. In adulthood there are other urgencies, and strokes are still important, but other urgencies must have higher priority. The condition of your belly has achieved top priority. Its blowout can literally cause you to bleed to death. Your belly's condition has the power of life or death, and you must pay proper attention, not to the pain but to the message in the pain.

STEVE: O.K. I'm prepared to listen.

INNER THERAPIST: Good. What has the belly been telling you?

BELLY: I'll speak for myself. Steve, you keep me in an uproar all the time. You roughen me up, shatter my lining, make my acids spurt out ferociously. You cause me to contract and you redden and bloody my walls. In short, you treat me the way you wouldn't dare treat anyone else in the world. And you force me to do what you wouldn't dream of doing.

STEVE: Whew! That's a big complaint.

INNER THERAPIST: Yes. Let's start by listening to it and see if it holds up. First, the roar in the uproar. It's true that you never roar—yell—at anyone. It's also true that many people in your life push you around and distress you, people you'd like to stand up to if you could be sure you wouldn't hurt their feelings and that they would continue to like you.

STEVE (*reluctantly*): Yes. As much as I hate to admit it, there are such people all around me—at home, in school, in my neighborhood.

INNER THERAPIST: Whenever they push you, you become even more placating. You make your stomach take responsibility for the pushiness you dare not show to the pushers around you. You make your stomach take responsibility for the rage you withdraw from. You make your stomach take responsibility for the hard contraction you refuse to express against all their inordinate demands and commands. You make your stomach bleed instead of acknowledging the bloody heads you'd like to bop.

STEVE (*putting his hands over his belly*): Oh, my poor belly. How much I've expected of you that I wouldn't dare express myself. (*Caresses his belly*)

BELLY: Yes, you have placed on me demands more outrageous than any demands those others ever placed on you.

STEVE (*still rubbing his belly*): Yes, I see that now. I've not really paid attention to you or your plight—only to the pain you caused me. I'll begin to listen more to you and to these things in my life you are teaching me to notice. (*Turns to the* INNER THERAPIST*)* How do I begin?

INNER THERAPIST: You've already begun. Look what you're doing— giving tenderness to your belly. Keep that up. The contact is important and it helps keep you in touch. That is the first step.

STEVE: Amazing! It actually feels better when I rub it like this. Such a simple device, and it's already working!

INNER THERAPIST: Fine. The other steps will entail considerable study. Get yourself a notebook. The questions you will have to ponder may be laborious. Often you'll wish you could just pop a pill and give up the labor. But if you stick to the task you'll be richly rewarded.

STEVE: Yes, I'm prepared to work. What kinds of questions do I begin with?

INNER THERAPIST: Let's start with pushiness. I'll spell out how to deal with this quality, then you can use the same design to deal with anger and rage.

Step One: Gently caress your belly, slowly, with open palms, softly and tenderly. There is healing power in your own hands. Use them, and don't be quick about it. Take your time.

Step Two: In your notebook, list all the people who push you around. Then describe in detail how they do this. Take your time. It's your earliest notebook assignment and requires considerable care. Give as many examples as possible for each person on your list. Don't worry about how long it takes. Just be

47

sure to deal with specific experiences and give a blow-by-blow description.

Step Three: Describe your feelings in each incident of being pushed. Go back to each experience you've listed in Step Two and see if you can reconstruct how you felt when you were pushed by a specific person in a specific way. You might have felt different when your principal pushed you around than when your sons did. Describe your feelings for each incident as concretely as possible.

Step Four: Describe your behavior in each incident. Again, be as detailed as possible. Did you smile, apologize for *their* pushing *you?* (Some people apologize when someone bumps into them.) Did you rush to rectify their complaint, or accede to their demand, or what?

Step Five: Starting today and for the remainder of this work keep a daily log of the foregoing assignments. Miracles sometimes do happen. You might find, with the growth of awareness resulting from these assignments, that the list of people who push you around, and the number of times they do it, will start to dwindle. Don't expect this to happen overnight, but one day, if you find you have no list to write, you'll know that the awareness itself helped resolve the problem. Don't forget, if *you* become aware of interpersonal assaults, your belly doesn't have to be aware for you and it can get back to its proper business. It won't have to hold the bag for you once you start holding your own bag.

Step Six: This will be the most difficult step of all—an assignment you won't do very well at first because you'll be too apt to censor things. But I'll give you the assignment anyway. When you get braver, you'll be able to carry it out properly, especially when you begin to trust me more after getting some good results from carrying out the previous assignments.

STEVE: Yes, go on. I'll do my best with Number Six.

INNER THERAPIST: First, I want to explain something to you about the mind. It is the one place in the world where utter freedom can be employed with the least destructiveness to anyone else. As a German song says, "Die Gedanken sind frei"—Thoughts are free. You may have heard it said that a virtuous person is not one who has no evil thoughts and impulses but rather one who does have these and who resists carrying them out. From this point of view we might say that you've thought only kindly

48

thoughts toward all your abusers and pushed the darker thoughts down into your belly's sac, making your belly contend with them because you would not acknowledge them. We must now reverse the process.

Now for Step Six. Go back and read the list of those pushy people in Step Two, then read the descriptions you've written of how they pushed you around. Read your feelings about being pushed around in Step Three. Now, after rereading those steps, allow yourself to have a fantasy or retaliation.

STEVE: But—

INNER THERAPIST: Ah, I told you this would be difficult for you. Bear the difficulty. Remember, if you are not free in your *thoughts,* where in the world can you be free? Remember also that *any fantasy*—no matter how bloody or gruesome—cannot hurt anybody else. The most dire deed done to bloodied victims in your fantasy will leave those persons smiling and going about their business, innocent of what they have just received in your thoughts. Your fantasy doesn't hurt them. And it will help you. It will relieve your belly from carrying the dark burden within its interior; free it to do its proper tasks; free you from repressed guilt as you learn to accept the tension of the darker side of your nature; and perhaps miraculously send the signal to those pushers that they'd better ease up. You might not have to raise a finger or even your voice to get these results. But you will need to raise your own pushy fantasies and feel your anxieties over harboring them within yourself. They are already in you. Releasing them to consciousness will free you and your stomach.

And I tell you it's all right—it's all right for you to *wish* to push back, even if you don't. It's all right for you to *wish* the abusers would disappear, even if you love them. It's all right for you to have bad thoughts, vengeful thoughts, even if you'd never carry them out. It's all right for you to be a human being with all the frailties and contradictions and good-mixed-with-evil impulses and thoughts that that entails.

STEVE *(sighs deeply):* Ohhh . . .

INNER THERAPIST: Yes, breathe deeply. Sigh for yourself. If you first allow yourself to sigh deeply for yourself, you'll be able to spare a sigh for all humanity.

CURTAIN

49

Steve sighs again, deeply. He is smiling. The belly smiles. The Inner Therapist smiles . . . as the curtain falls.

THE END

You've just witnessed the initial steps toward understanding the ulcer. If you're suffering from a gastric or duodenal ulcer, awareness of the language of the ulcerous belly is of prime importance. You've seen how this language, which describes your belly's state, may be a reflection of your actual state in the outside world. And finally, you've seen how arduous it is to study not the belly's state but your own state, to study the nature of your responses, both fully conscious and those you may be dimly and ashamedly aware of. This is your proper study if you are to reclaim your own responsibility for your behavior, if you are to stop using your belly for a dumping ground.

And don't forget the first and easiest step of all, even if you feel foolish doing it—a simple, gentle, caring caress. Remember, a small touch goes a long, long way. And your belly, which you may have abused in greater or lesser degree than did Steve, is in *need* of your attention. There is no one in the world, no medical doctor of even great renown, no medication, that can give your belly the solace and care it needs for proper functioning.

You alone can do this.

You are *it,* the proper nourisher, the proper caretaker. To prove this thesis, to show how important you are to your belly (ulcer or no) and how your belly—like a loved dog—will respond, to prove this, just touch your belly gently right now with full, open-palmed contact and rub it gently back and forth . . . slowly . . . slowly . . . remembering to sigh deeply . . . more deeply. Use both open palms. Be nice to your stomach, especially you who have trained yourself and been trained by others to *be nice* to so many others in your life. Take these few minutes to be nice to your own stomach and feel its response. Feel it. It is your best reward.

4
Position Is Everything in Life

You have to dissemble. . . . It's necessary in order to get into office and in order to retain office.

—*Richard Nixon,*
in an interview on Good Morning, America,
as reported in Welcomat
(Philadelphia), Nov. 3, 1982

Truth has no formula.
—*Socrates*

The continuance in this vile habit [bad posture] will certainly produce a consumption [tuberculosis].

—*Aaron Burr*
to his daughter Theodosia in 1790.
From Mary Cable, The Little Darlings

"Stand up straight, stop hunching over. Do you want to be a hunchback!" Oh how many children, with these phrases hurled at them in exasperation or anger, have crumbled under the assaults? How many would not, could not, ever learn to stand up straight and would carry these assaults within themselves for a lifetime and go to their ultimate graves with bowed backs and bowed spirits?

Actually, it's just as easy to stand up straight and tall, and it's more pleasurable. It's just as easy to breathe deeply without the bowing over. Why, then, are there so many bowed backs? Except for the relatively few of us with congenital defects, we don't start out that way, certainly not since Neanderthal times.

Evidently we are evolutionarily designed for the upright position—maybe to keep that most vulnerable (and potentially danger-ous) part of our anatomy, the brain, aloft and free from harm. Or maybe to elevate it above the level of our genitals, as if some special meaning for the human being is thereby intended.

One can go on speculating about the whys and wherefores, but it's clearly observed that the healthy stance for the human being *is* that very stance which our parents have insisted upon. Then why do so many, especially in their early teens, look as though they'd like to resume the position of the four-legged species? Why do so many assume bowed positions, which inhibit breathing and diminish a sense of well-being?

If you don't think the bowed position of your back has these plaguey results, try it. Curve your back forward in an exaggerated hump and take as deep a breath as you can. Take a few. See how tough it is to take a satisfying full breath?

And now sit or stand up with regal stature—not stiff but tall. Exaggerate the stature, the elongated height, and take as deep a breath as you can in this position. Slowly take a few more.

See what I mean? The expansive feeling of well-being? You might even find a smile on your face. Good—leave it there, and keep breathing. Such fringe benefits should be welcomed. They're few enough and far enough between.

Then how come, if uprightness is so pleasurable, so many of us bow over? I am now going to commit an unconscionable act—I'm going to blame our parents for starting our backs on their downward curve. Well, why not? After all, we owe our genes to them, we owe our material inheritance to them, why not our positions as well?

Let's see if this theory of indebtedness holds up. It certainly applies in Marjorie's case. Marjorie's daughter was a sturdy child with broad, straight shoulders who maintained an almost perfect posture throughout her toddler phase. Then Marjorie divorced her husband after learning he was having an affair with her neighbor, a divorcée. Changing from an interested parent, though somewhat permissive, Marjorie began to feel a growing impatience and frus-tration with her daughter, which reflected a more general frustra-tion in her own life. She became more and more critical and, while she never struck little Emily physically, she hurled barrages of complaints at her. At first Emily cried and cried, which only exasperated her mother more. Then Emily gradually began to bow her body forward. It was as if her body were ashamed of itself, ashamed of its very existence. After all, her father had lived happily with her mother before she was born—didn't her mother often enough tell her stories of her life before Emily? And didn't Emily's father leave her mother after Emily's birth? Clearly it was all her fault that her father left. There must be some terrible thing about her that caused him to leave her mother. No wonder her mother was so angry with her.

And, with a clarity of perception and certainty that comes readily to a child, Emily understood her mother's blame and criticism as being therefore justified, and her shame grew. With each of her mother's verbal assaults the shame, like a millstone around Emily's neck, pulled her self-esteem lower and lower until her shoulders followed, and Emily's esteem and her back bowed over in unison. By the time Emily was ten, her mother had to seek orthopedic help for her.

Now, all of us who are bowed over do not come from broken homes or yelling mothers—at least not obviously, as in Emily's case. Our stories are not so pat and comprehensible. They lurk in the shadows with hidden connections. And it does not help very much to say: "Yes, but my brothers and sisters don't have bowed backs—so why do I? It can't be my mother's fault or all of us kids would have the same condition."

Not so. No two children in a family have the same parents, with perhaps the exception of identical twins.

The first child in a family is born to parents of a specific age who are virginal about parenting, uncertain, inexperienced with the right and wrong way of bringing up baby. Therefore, most mistakes are perpetrated on that first child. And, with the birth of that child, the most radical change takes place in the parents' lives. They are instantly catapulted from the two of their own company to the crowd of three, and they must now contend, for the first time in their relationship, with their new threesome.

Also, most of the parents' excitements and enthusiasms as well as their relative youth are presented to the firstborn. Never again will such a mixture of fears, ignorance, hope, excitement, ecstasy, and uncertainty be showered on an offspring from that union. Never again will the parents be so *young*.

The second child is born to parents who are older than the birth-time parents of the first child, born to parents who have already parented. The second child comes into a *family* of *three*; the first into a union of two adults. The second child has an older sibling. The first is an only child and then must give the single status over to the younger sibling. Each of these differences in these tender and most impressionable years—more impressionable than at *any* subsequent time—has *mammoth* consequences. Thus, my contention that no children born into a family at different times come from the *same* parents or the *same* family.

And because of the uniqueness of each person's burden, no generalized remedy exists for bowed backs. Each back bows to its unique burdens, burdens as unique as fingerprints.

Some people, instead of bowing over, go in the opposite direction and hold their bodies as erect as though a steel poker replaced their spine and a crossbar their shoulders—the military stance, frozen in position, never at ease. Many people with this body position are holding in an underlying depression; the steel rods not only form a cross on which they are crucified but also are the sluice gates holding back their flood of unfelt tears. While the cause is uniquely determined, at least one generality can be made: These people frequently soften their steel-like structural rigidity when they undergo a baptism with their unshed tears by allowing the flood to erupt.

Sometimes, instead of the bowing forward or the rigidifying of the spine and shoulders, there is an abnormal curvature of the spine to one side, a condition known as scoliosis which usually starts early in life. Scoliosis, in its milder forms, is a common cause of lower back pain; in its more severe forms, it causes the malfunction of internal organs, including vital organs like the lungs.

Why does the spine twist over into a lateral curve? Since no one knows for sure, it's anybody's guess. My guess goes something like this: since the body's right and left sides do not grow in unison (at any one time before the bones are fused and the body stops growing, one leg or arm will be shorter than the other—that is, each side does not grow simultaneously with its opposite side), and since at any time we can be stuck in the position we find ourselves (stuck in an emotional state, stuck in a psychological developmental state), and since our bodies often reflect our state of being stuck, then if a psychological trauma happens at a time when the body's two sides are unequal, it seems not unlikely that the body can get stuck in the physical position it happens to be in when the particular trauma occurs. Then, when the other side grows, the body is even more

54

unbalanced, and the curve toward the shorter side becomes more pronounced.

This would be difficult to prove without getting together a group of children with scoliosis and helping them tune in to their Inner Therapists, who could help them confront these traumatic conditions that may have stuck them in their curved positions. I wish somebody would try it out.

Again, the presence of the Inner Therapist is a general, a universal condition. The *dialogue* with the Inner Therapist and the resulting insights and discoveries are *specific* and *individual*. These cannot be bottled or put out in the form of a mass-produced pill. Your own Inner Therapist is in the world in a special way only for you, for your needs. It assists you partly because it is uniquely attentive to *you.*

Do you have a distorted body position? Through that very distortion your Inner Therapist speaks to you.

Is your body asymmetrical? Does one eyebrow stick up higher than the other? Does one side of your mouth curve down lower than the other? What, through your asymmetry, is your Inner Therapist saying to you?

This brings to mind Mike, a young hood in jail for multiple burglaries and threatening a store owner with a knife. Mike's history was typical of many of his slum peers: mother on welfare, too many kids in the family and thus overcrowded tenement living, father a demoralized alcoholic who beat the children when he was around, which wasn't often until he finally vamoosed altogether.

Mike's face was asymmetrical because of the way his mouth curled down at the right corner of his lip. Even when he smiled, that corner of his lip looked as though it might want to go up like the other side but was pulled downward as if a hook and anchor hung on it. When he talked, he actually talked out of the hole his lips made on the right side—he literally talked out of the side of his mouth.

Now, if you have a condition of asymmetry—and you don't have to be a criminal to be so afflicted, there are lots of asymmetrical law-abiding people walking freely around—you might think of the one side *in relation* to the other side. It's the sameness or difference between the two sides that makes for the presence or absence of symmetry, and it is this difference we must confront in order to gain any understanding of the meaning or message underlying the asymmetry.

Let's take Mike's asymmetrical corners of his lips and see if their dialogue can give us a clue to the purpose or message for Mike in this asymmetry.

We'll start, as usual, with a self-description of the part, keeping in mind that in the case of asymmetry it is a description of the one side *relative* to the other side. This dialogue is not easy to achieve in Mike's case. He is not used to getting close to himself or his body parts. He has drugged his brain at every possible opportunity. He has sought distance, not closeness. It would take some heavy-duty doing to get Mike, or anyone like him, to become intimate with himself or anyone else. After all, getting close to his father usually meant getting a beating. But, assuming some cooperation, the dialogue might run this way:

RIGHT CORNER OF LIP (*to* LEFT CORNER): I jut out. I'm lower than you. Almost never as high as you and never, never higher. But even though I'm lower, Mike does most of his talking through me, on my side. So, you might be on a higher level, but I've won his speech over to my side.

LEFT CORNER: I am normal, I'm on a normal level. I'm not distorted like you. I'm not scrunched together like you. When Mike smiles, I turn upward like I'm supposed to and give a pleasant look on my side. You are gruesome and ridiculous. I'm higher than you. You're always curled down low, as if you're always set on going down to the basement. I stay here on an even keel. You make Mike look like an inmate who has to talk on the side of his mouth to the other convicts so the guards don't hear.

RIGHT CORNER: So where did your being on the level get you? You're still locked up in jail with Mike, just like I am. And look how uptight you are—always closed up. Even when Mike talks, you're closed up like a clam. Me, I'm always open. I'm low but at least I move.

LEFT CORNER: There's no point talking to you. I should have known better than to start up with you.

RIGHT CORNER: That's it, Lefty, blame it all on me. Just like you to cast the blame around.

IMPASSE

MIKE: I can never keep the corners of my lips level with each other. Ha! That's a good one! I've been in rackets all my life and even my lips aren't on the level. Hahahahaha!

56

Mike is known as a psychopath or, synonymously, a sociopath. Let us digress and ask what is a psychopath or sociopath anyway? The term "psychopath" is the one previously used by psychiatrists for someone exhibiting persistent antisocial behavior, but since it became part of the language of the street, the term "sociopath" replaced it—perhaps to guard the mystique of professional language from invasion by the populace. I will use the terms interchangeably. In order to get a handle on Mike and his asymmetry, it would help if we understood the label the authorities pinned on him.

The usual stance of the usual psychopath can be characterized by the statement, "I want what I want when I want it." Psychopaths brook no interference with their wants. In this regard they are like the infant who will screech and carry on in the middle of the night, waking up the entire household if necessary to get its urges and needs satisfied. The infant has no concern for anyone else's comfort, convenience, pleasure, desires, needs. The world revolves around only one set of impulses and needs—the infant's. It is the same with psychopaths. The world is their oyster and should crack its own shell open for the psychopath's ease and convenience. Expediency in getting wants fulfilled is the sociopath's top priority, and laws are made for fools to follow and for the sociopath to despise.

Failure to experience conscience, a lack of feeling or empathy for others, characterizes the psychopath. The psychopath is always *me first*, whereas the person of highly developed social conscience puts the *conscience* first, even before physical safety of the self.

The typical psychopath harbors one fear more excruciating than any other. Can you guess what it is? No, it is not fear of getting caught or killed. Of these things psychopaths tend to have a *lower* than usual quotient of fear. In fact, many psychopaths seem to set themselves up to assure getting caught.

You or I might feel instantaneous shame if caught in some misdeed. Not so the psychopath. What for most of us would make us want to crawl into a hole if caught in our commission of our "crime" for the psychopath is a point of honor and pride. "Ha! I did it! So what!"

Although the shocking crimes of mass killers make the headlines, most psychopaths are not killers. And this "diagnosis," like all psychiatric diagnoses (My book *Don't Shrink to Fit!* [Grove Press, 1976] describes the harmfulness of psychiatric diagnoses), fails to be helpful because most people at some time commit sociopathic acts,

acts that go against the social good for the benefit of the individual. The criminal psychopath is merely an extreme degree of a tendency in all of us—some more, some less. As psychiatrist Harry Stack Sullivan said, we are all more alike than different.

But the extreme psychopath who chronically lies, steals, cheats, or kills and is proud of what he or she can get away with, what can cause that person *shame?*

Most of us in this country think in terms of socially acceptable behavior, social "norms" of the Judeo-Christian ethic and morality. And it is precisely those very *norms* of behavior, of proper conduct, of honest dealings, that cause such grief to the psychopath. If you asked average persons to picture themselves stealing something from a store, then getting caught and being publicly exposed, they would feel anxiety and shameful embarrassment. Not so with extreme psychopaths, who, conversely, would suffer anxiety and shame if they had to picture themselves acting in a socially acceptable way. They literally break out in a cold sweat. The Judeo-Christian code is all right for the rest of society, those who want to be led or fleeced, but not for these master manipulators. They shudder, literally, at the mere thought of conforming.

I remember Chuck, a long-haired college student who came to see me in the early 1970s. He had been caught dealing with dope in school. Actually, he wasn't going to profit from the deal himself, he was just doing a friend a favor and was putting two people together—a buyer and a seller. Except that the buyer happened to be an undercover agent.

Before Chuck was to appear in court for his trial, his lawyer ordered him to get his hair cut to impress the judge with his "normality."

Chuck was very upset—not because he'd lose his tousled locks, but because he couldn't stand the thought of *looking normal.* It freaked him out to think of what his freaky friends would think of him! His deepest shame was for his peers to see him with "normal" hair. This was worse to bear than the thought of going to jail, disgracing his family, getting kicked out of school, etc. He would gladly have had his jail sentence doubled—anything, anything, rather than be seen as *straight, conforming,* fitting the *norm.* And Chuck was not even particularly psychopathic. Just enough to give us some idea of how *awful* a sensation it is when the psychopath thinks about conforming.

And now, with this added understanding, we can get back to Mike and his asymmetrical lips. Recall that the two corners of his lips—the left straight or level, the right jutting down under—have just reached an impasse in their attempted dialogue. And, at that point of no return, a turning becomes possible with the advent of Mike's Inner Therapist. The following scene shows Mike, the level left corner, the low-down right corner, and the Inner Therapist. Mike is so far removed from his inner *anything* that one might say he has put his Inner Therapist in jail and thrown away the key.

LEFT CORNER: It's not fair. They're taking unfair advantage of me. It's two against one.
INNER THERAPIST: How so?
LEFT CORNER: Mike favors his lip's right corner. That leaves me out in the cold.
MIKE: Hey, knock it off. My lips are my lips—right side, left side, inside and outside.
INNER THERAPIST: Mike, when you abuse any part of your body, or neglect it or insult it, it acts like any abused child will act. It gets sullen, withdraws into itself, plots its revenge to get back at you and do you harm.
MIKE: Aw, I don't have no trouble with my body. I don't know what you're even talking about.
    (Another impasse—total denial)

The undaunted Inner Therapist continues.
INNER THERAPIST: All right, you say you have no trouble with your body. But your body is in jail right now. You say that your being in jail doesn't give you any trouble?
MIKE: Aw, the stupid judge, he didn't know his knee from his elbow. And my lawyer fouled up too. But I won't be here much longer.
    (The denial continues . . .)
INNER THERAPIST: Then you have no trouble at all?
MIKE: Nah. I could do with a smoke or a joint, though.
INNER THERAPIST *(persisting)*: So you have no trouble at all?
MIKE: What are you, some broken record or something? C'mon. Bug out of here.
INNER THERAPIST: One more thing. Why are your lips different? Why does your right corner go down like that?
MIKE: It's a habit. Maybe I saw a gangster movie when I was a kid and saw Edward G. Robinson talk that way once. How should I

59

know? I know only one thing—you're bugging me with all these stupid questions.

INNER THERAPIST: You've got that backward, Mike. It's you who are bugging me, and bugging yourself in the process. Now, you'd better listen to me, because I'm all you've got.

MIKE: What'ya mean, you're all I got? I've got myself. I don't need you or anybody else.

INNER THERAPIST: You're wrong about that. You don't have yourself. You're separated from yourself. You abuse yourself. You drug your brain cells any chance you get, because not only are you not close to yourself, but you can't seem to stand the feelings that go with getting close to yourself. You contort your mouth to fit some phony criminal ideal of yours. Then when your separation from yourself becomes unbearable, you do something to get thrown in jail, where at least you're locked up with yourself and can't physically run off in all directions.

So here you are now . . . and if you'd listen to your own body's distortions, there'd be a powerful message there for you, more powerful than any drug trip you've taken your brain cells on.

MIKE: All right, all right. I'll listen, I'll listen.

INNER THERAPIST: Good. Now, the sides of your mouth are asymmetrical, the left level, the right down. These two corners, believe it or not, reflect aspects of yourself. In your life you've acted like your right lip: curved down, strained, an underdog. Your left corner is level, on the level, straight—a condition you've never experienced, certainly not since you were a child and began to develop the angles, angling at first how to get out of the beatings, out of the being pushed around.

Maybe if you had been straight with your father, he'd have knocked your block off, so working the angles may have saved your life at that time. But now, being on the level or being straight is not only what you *choose* not to be but something you can't stand to be, something you're *afraid* to be.

MIKE: It's got nothing to do with what I can't stand. Being straight just don't pay off, that's all. I can make more in one quick trip to Mexico—just one quick trip—than I could make working on the level for a whole year. I'd be a number-one jerk to work at an ordinary job every day for a year when I can make a killing on one single drug deal in one day. I'd be a real creep to go straight.

INNER THERAPIST: If you're not afraid, let's see you prove it.

MIKE: Prove it? What'ya mean?

INNER THERAPIST: If you think being on the level is so easy for you, try it.

MIKE: Yeah. Just get me out of here and I'll show you what I can do.

INNER THERAPIST: I have no power to get you out of here. That's not my precinct. The only power I have is to show you how you are—how you kid yourself, lie to yourself, do a number on yourself, how you don't own up to what you're really up to, what you really need, and how you are and aren't satisfying your needs.

MIKE: Yeah, well if you're so smart, you show me. Go on—show me what I'm really up to. Go on.

INNER THERAPIST: You really want me to?

MIKE: I really want you to shut up. But if you're gonna stick around giving me your lip, then go on, talk and get it over with.

INNER THERAPIST: Then you'll listen?

MIKE: Yeah, yeah. Just get it over with, will ya?

INNER THERAPIST: Then you'll have to keep quiet and *listen*. That's not easy for you. You're always so busy working the angles, plotting the shots, figuring how to strike a hit, that you have trouble *listening*. So, for starters, keep your mouth shut and your eyes and ears open.

MIKE: All right already . . . but don't keep your own trap open so much. There's too much hot air in here already. Move on with it. What'ya want me to listen to?

INNER THERAPIST: First, when did you decide that doing things the straight way didn't pay off? How early in your life did you stop being on the level?

MIKE (shouting): Hey, what's that got to do with anything? I'm not here to get into any psychology junk. My past has nothing to do with it.

INNER THERAPIST: Maybe so, but then, maybe not. Let's just get into it a little and poke around. I'm not interested in psychoanalyzing you. I just want to look for *connections*, and I need your help.

MIKE: Well, I can't help you with anything. My past is for me to know and for you to find out. Besides, I don't remember too much about it, and I don't want to bother my head about it. So move on to the next point.

INNER THERAPIST: Mike, it's best if we start at the beginning. Then we can understand what caused later things that have come up.

MIKE (angry): I told you I'm not gonna bother with any of that!

61

There was nothing wrong with my childhood. Nothing. Everything was A-O.K.

INNER THERAPIST: Whenever anyone gets as hot as you're getting about this, you can be sure there's a fire there somewhere. C'mon, Mike, let's investigate the fire together so it doesn't keep burning you.

MIKE: Knock it off, I said. If you don't shut your trap about it right now, I'll . . .

INNER THERAPIST: Mike, who made you eat humble pie? Who poured hot pepper on your tongue? Who beat you till your skin was raw and bleeding?

MIKE: Hey, bug off I said! I'm warning you. You want to talk about today, O.K., but no yesterdays. That's it. That's my last warning.

INNER THERAPIST: All right, we'll stick to today. But I have a hunch you won't talk about that either. You won't let anything get near you or touch you.

MIKE: Try me, try me. You'll see.

INNER THERAPIST: Mike, I don't think you can picture yourself acting like your left lip—on the level.

MIKE: Why should I? I told you already, it don't pay off.

INNER THERAPIST: I'm not telling you to *do* it—just to *picture* it.

MIKE (*menacingly*): Knock it off, I said.

INNER THERAPIST: What are you getting so hot about? I'm simply suggesting a fantasy—a picture of your acting straight, on the level.

MIKE (*in a violent outburst*): Get out of here! I won't take any more! Go on . . . beat it . . . right now!

Mike, menacing, refuses to go on. The mere suggestion of turning his mind on the straight and narrow path throws him into an uproar that neatly covers up his dread of straight, on-the-level behavior. The mere idea throws him into a tailspin, which he gets out of only by threatening to erupt into violent behavior—the behavior of the underworld, where to be crossed or double-crossed invites violent retribution.

Mike shows here another characteristic of the psychopathic pattern: the inability to suffer any anxiety. Tough as he is, this is one thing he can't take on the chin. With the slightest tinge of anxiety his fists are up, ready to fight; he is ready to leap into action and ward off the *feel* of the anxiety. As I've said, the factor causing the largest degree of anxiety to the psychopath is the picture of going straight, like the left corner of Mike's lip.

Then what's the solution for Mike and other so-called psychopaths? It's a slow process because of their intolerance to anxiety. Tranquilizers and other drugs only delay the necessary confrontation and thus make things worse, not better. Such people have to learn little by little to suffer the tension of their own anxiety, learn that they can survive the lack of instant gratification, that they don't die if they don't get their symbolic bottle or breast on the spot. It's a slow, step-by-step proposition, whereby people like Mike can learn to reclaim their own anxiety and live side by side with it.

Instead of dishing out the drugs or tranquilizers, Hamlet's advice would be more efficacious:

> Refrain tonight,
> And that shall lend a kind of easiness
> To the next abstinence; the next more easy;
> For use almost can change the stamp of nature.
> (Act 3, Scene 4)

So if you tend toward psychopathic behavior and want to do something about it, listen to Hamlet's advice—refrain this once from your urge toward gratification at all costs—just once—and feel the valor of that conquest over blind obedience to your impulses. Feel the strength in that resistance. Feel the anxiety—it is your friend, your protector.

Feel the anxiety, feel the tremendous *excitement* released. Let yourself feel the force behind that anxiety. The force is there for you to use in ways you've never dreamed of. Ironically, you'll need that force to face the greatest anxiety of all—the anxiety of conformity, of legitimacy, of being and acting on the level. If you don't believe that the mere thought of "straight" behavior can make you break out in a cold sweat if you are sociopathic, try to imagine it right now. Picture yourself doing socially acceptable deeds and see how long you can stand it without your heart beginning to pound, your breath coming in short gasps, your palms perspiring.

Why have I spent so much time on the psychopath? Aren't most of us law-abiding citizens? Socially useful? Charitable? If there's any lesson we can learn from Watergate, it is that the danger that the psychopathic condition will impregnate the very fiber of American life is a real and present danger. And if it happens "out there," it is not just some fluke that has nothing to do with us. If it's happening anywhere out there, it's also happening in some ways in our own homes, right before our eyes.

I hope I have managed in some small measure to raise questions that are well worth your asking. And I hope your Inner Therapist will be a more successful guide to *your* asymmetries than Mike's was to his.

5
Messages from Inside

O the mind, mind has mountains; cliffs of fall
Frightful, sheer, no-man-fathomed. Hold them cheap
May who ne'er hung there.
—*Gerard Manley Hopkins,*
"No Worst, There Is None"

We are never single-minded, unperplexed, like migratory birds.
—*Rainer Maria Rilke,* Duino Elegies, IV

Water silently moves in to fill
The contours
And empty spaces.
—*Elizabeth Coleman,*
"The Bath"

"What messages are in your stories?" Isaac Bashevis Singer was asked by a member of the audience at the University of Pennsylvania on April 23, 1979. He answered: "One good story has a hundred messages. You can have a hundred messages without one good story. I try to write a good story."

We are inundated with messages that need deciphering, and our job is to find the story line that connects them into a relevant whole, so that we can know ourselves and learn the essential messages of our life-line.

Our minds receive messages from our bodies—diverse messages.

Our minds deliver messages to our bodies—a complexity and perplexity of messages.

Unlike migratory birds who follow one voice with single-minded purpose, the bodies of us human beings are anything but single-voiced.

In the birds' domain, a unilateral commandment, *"Go south!"* mobilizes the flocks, gets them into proper position, fills the skies in precision formation, and presto!—they zoom, unswerving, to their destination.

But we human beings hear many commandments, opposing voices vibrating in different rhythms, conflicting with one another. We are walking towers of Babel. The head says *no,* the heart says *yes,* the stomach says *now,* the bowel says *later*—simultaneously!

It's one of the miracles of the human organism that our multilingual minds, hearts, and bodies—going in opposing directions at one and the same time (the brain itself dividing with opposing right-left intent)—can somehow be decoded by a central inner mechanism into a coherent structure that prevents us from flying off in all directions at once.

Early in our lives, many choices and options are trained out of us, but we still have lots to spare. And *it is our ability to make choices that remains one of our most valuable human characteristics.* When winter comes we don't *have* to fly south—we can choose to stay north. We can survive and thrive in winter's domain.

As with all the rest of the paradoxical nature of humankind, it is this very choice-making that gives us so much trouble—so much trouble, in fact, that many human beings are content to give up this vital human characteristic and docilize themselves into cowness. You might say they are so cowed by the fact of the human condition that they willingly transform themselves into cowhood.

Lest you think I am exaggerating the danger of *your* joining the bovines, consider what you did recently when you felt anxious. Consider what you did with even the earliest tinge of tension, or even when you merely thought you *might* get anxious. If you did what all too many Americans do under such circumstances, you undoubtedly reached for a tranquilizer or a sedative or some other pill to docilize your tensions, bovinize your conflicts—in an attempt to remove yourself securely and contentedly from having to make a *choice* about the source of your disturbance.

Tranquilizing the brain is tantamount to putting your ability to make choices out to pasture.

In a recent television appearance where I was discussing the psychological aspects of obesity in my book *Fat Chance,* two obesity sufferers joined the discussion. One, a woman, had had her stomach stapled, and she said she was happy because her man-made small stomach prevented her from eating as much as she used to and it was "such a relief not to have to choose anymore."

The other, a 350-pound man with a jolly smile, said he loved to eat and his weight didn't bother him at all, but that he had decided to go on a special diet program in which every meal was prepackaged and all he had to do was eat the contents of the packages and nothing else. "What a relief not having to choose what to eat!" he beamed.

The easiest thing to do is to still the voice of the symptom—anesthetize it, reach for a drug, kill it. But then, going downhill always is easier. Death is peaceful, easier than life. If you're committed to the easy-death process, you'll continue to stock your medicine cabinet and your body with tranquilizers.

But if you want to *live* your life, then struggle, conflict, and anxiety will be your necessary companions—else, what's an adrenal for?

I don't mean we should accept our suffering, resign ourselves to it, glory in it, do nothing to change it. No, this resignation is another way, although more subtle, of not heeding the body's voice.

The pain, the conflict, the anxiety, the racing heart, and the pounding head must be acknowledged, heard. "What are they telling us?" we must ask. "What must I understand about my life? In what way are my symptoms important harbingers, messengers of my life? What do they foretell of the tower I must build?"

Questions must be asked. We need to ask more questions—not rush pell-mell to solve everything with our ready-made answers, our deadly solutions, our quick, destructive cures. Life is crying to be *heard,* not cured.

Let us now hear what some people with common symptoms learned when they began to listen to their inner voices.

Joyce, a thirty-year-old married woman, had had premenstrual tensions and abdominal pains for years. The pains would begin about two weeks prior to every menstrual period and continue until her period began. She had made the round of gynecologists, internists, and general surgeons and tried medications and diets—all to no avail. Some doctors even suggested that she get pregnant as the solution. In the back of her mind she feared having a baby just to cure herself, felt she was the type to develop a postpartum depression and go bonkers altogether.

When Joyce began talking to her Inner Therapist, she asked, "What is happening in my life every time I start to develop my symptoms?" and came up readily with the answer: "The pains begin when I'm in the middle of my menstrual cycle. I'm ovulating!"

This "revelation" opened a Pandora's box. Through a series of associations, ovulation for Joyce meant first and foremost that she was a woman, female—a condition that, despite her marriage, she had *never* been happy about. Once she opened up the pains of being female, she let out the harsh relationship with her abusive mother, who demeaned her at every turn. As if for the first time, Joyce heard the love-hate conflicts with her mother, her desperate yearnings to get her mother's approval for *female* things. And once these repressed voices were heard, Joyce's abdominal pains, which had plagued her for over a dozen years, cleared up. *They were no longer necessary.* She had heard their voices.

Serge, at age twenty-eight, had "tension headaches," but because he had to live up to a certain image, he never took time off from work. He was afraid to, felt he had to make a good impression on his boss. As a result, he drove himself fiercely, often working overtime while his head pounded away, and when the weekend came around, instead of going out with friends to enjoy some leisure, he'd wind up in bed with an ice pack on his head.

When Serge described his symptoms in dialogue with his Inner Therapist, he took the part of those symptoms and stated:

"Like a mallet I pound Serge's head. I keep pounding away. I don't stop."

One word led to another and led Serge back to his father's drumming in the message of taking punishment like a "man" (at age three). "Big boys don't cry," "Be obedient," "Follow orders," "Have good manners."

Serge was *mortified* to learn how many "pounding" impulses he had against that big, powerful, righteous father of his, impulses Serge never even dared bring to consciousness, impulses reactivated in his relationship with his big, powerful boss. Serge's own conflicts with his forbidden impulses to hammer his boss's (father's) head in cleared up, not by knocking his boss's brains out, but by merely bringing these impulses to his own awareness—that is, by listening to his body's voice, the voice of his symptoms, listening to his Inner Therapist using whatever means at hand, even painful head-pounding ones, to wake Serge up to his life's condition. And, when he came to consciousness and no longer needed the extreme pounding to wake him up, Serge's chronic headaches vanished.

But is it *always* related to these early relationships, even symptoms that don't start until middle age? The answer is a resounding *YES, always!* Always? Well, almost always.

For instance, Wendy, age sixty-one, had suffered from severe multiple allergies for five years. She had the help of the best allergists from the most prestigious medical centers, but despite tests, desensitization shots, medications, and dietary restrictions, she was fast becoming an invalid. Whenever she went out to eat—in restaurants or at friends'—she carried her "permissible" foods with her, which were becoming more and more restricted. If she dared digress from her severely limited dietary regime, her tongue would catch fire, her eyes would get bloodshot, her stomach would knot— she'd be a total wreck.

Starting by describing one of her most distressing symptoms—her burning tongue—Wendy took the part of the tongue and these words emerged: "I burn. I cause pain. I am red hot, fierce." One word leading to a volume with the help of a dialogue with her Inner Therapist, it was revealed that Wendy was always afraid of her mother and had always been cold to her. Wendy, however, despite her coldness was a most dutiful daughter and tried never to cause her mother any trouble. But Wendy paid the price of such duty—she developed a cold indifference which surrounded her heart, an indifference she carried with her into her marriage and her relationships with her three daughters.

Wendy never knew how much passionate hatred—fiery hate— smoldered all those years under her dutiful deference to her mother. This condition was never uncovered until her Inner Therapist with the metaphorical symptom of the burning tongue led the way.

And then—what fierce rages, buried under all those years of cold, dutiful indifference, poured out! Burning words of hate and accusation and passionate blame spurted forth. Wendy allowed it all to reach first her consciousness and then the air. She lashed out, sparking, but not without shame, guilt, and humiliation. The conflict with her mother, so long repressed and now brought to light, was *raw*, hurting. But it was confronted and finished with. And she recalled her mother's fiery tongue-lashings, which Wendy had long ago forgotten.

Now her tongue no longer had to burn. Miraculously, Wendy began eating all the foods that had once distressed her. Moreover, for the first time in her life, she began to *feel something* positive for her mother, some loving and caring feelings. These feelings did not go unnoticed by her eighty-five-year-old mother, who, warmed by the genuine expression of real tenderness from her daughter, began to say the endearing things she had never in her life expressed, phrases which nurtured the empty places inside Wendy.

These two elderly women, cold, distant, polite with each other for over half a century, began to nourish one another and heat the winter's breath in their lives.

Wendy's contact with her rage, thanks to her unsentimental and objective Inner Therapist, had paradoxically thawed her ice-caked heart and allowed her loving sentiments to flow.

You may complain: "That's hard to swallow! Do you mean to say Wendy knew *nothing* of her hate or anger for her mother during all those years of her life?" And I must answer, "Yes, that's exactly what I mean, even though it's almost not to be believed." Moreover, Wendy is not *exceptional* in this.

Over and over again I meet people whose most obvious sentiment, justified by an objective point of view, is barricaded away from themselves, camouflaged underneath some symptom and kept out of reach of their wildest imaginings. It's always a great revelation when these people uncover feelings they have harbored for a lifetime. And when they do so, they no longer need the symptoms they have created to conceal those underlying feelings.

You might well ask, "But why is this so? Why do we have to develop cover-ups, symptoms, instead of feeling our feelings in the first place?"

There are some feelings that for a variety of reasons are excruciating for us. They may be feelings that are fundamentally forbidden, urges that are intolerable and overwhelming, thoughts that threaten our equilibrium and would cause panic and dread if brought to the surface. And to keep ourselves in some state of balance, we learn to shy away from these feelings, we learn how to lock them up so securely that we hardly know they exist.

But our feelings don't go away when they're locked up. They wait. We spend a lot of our energy keeping them out of sight, under lock and key, while they wait, ready to leap out as soon as we open the door.

In the meantime, to keep them hidden away we develop symptoms or camouflages that not only help disguise our real feelings but also in some way remind us that they're still there waiting for release. Those disowned feelings, thoughts, and urges can outwait all our attempts to incarcerate them, and thus through the medium of our symptoms we are kept from abandoning them altogether.

In this Pill Age, dedicated to exterminating symptoms under the guise of "cure," the concept of the symptom as camouflage *and* connector is difficult to swallow. We've been brainwashed to reach for the nearest dearest pill and get rid of everything the least bit unpleasant—even the dearest parts of ourselves, the connecting links with the human condition: our feelings.

In the next chapter we'll talk about feelings that we know about, feelings that have surfaced and that we are in contact with. Here I'm referring mostly to forbidden feelings that we do not dare let up for air, feelings that we stringently keep stifled in the darkest cell of our innermost chambers. To reconnect with them and the thoughts and urges they engender, to recognize them as a dear and important part of our selves, we must pay the cost of experiencing dread or anxiety. And when you think of the rich value in achieving human status you might shoulder the cost with forbearance.

What is the nature of the feelings we keep locked up at the cost of such an energy drain to our selves? And what can be so dreadful to face that we must keep them submerged so deep?

Millicent's Inner Therapist gives us a clue when she confronts a disturbing symptom. Millicent's nose had been fine and well-behaved until sometime after she started to work as a junior executive for her father's New York firm. The job carried with it a lot of responsibility, which Millicent handled efficiently and capably.

Then Millicent developed a singular symptom—a nose that kept running. It ran and it ran. Doctors could neither discover the cause nor find a cure.

Millicent was a twenty-eight-year-old college graduate, bright and personable. Her blue eyes sparkled with enthusiasm and vitality. Her father, an erratic domineering egomaniac, insisted she leave her job working at the college and come to work in his business.

Millicent dutifully submitted, but her father's wild mood swings and incessant and unreasonable demands almost drove her crazy. He was never satisfied with anything she did, and she was stuck on the treadmill of knocking herself out trying to please him and yet always seeming to incur his raging complaints. On the rare occasions when he would compliment Millicent, he would turn around the next minute and criticize her for the very thing that had just elicited the compliment.

Millicent loved her father—and hated him—in a wild mixture that kept her constantly on edge, expecting the worst whenever she was in his presence, or even when she merely thought about him. Her stomach would knot up and she would get feelings of pressure in her head. It was clear that these symptoms were related to the pressures put on her by that erratic father of hers.

But when she was away from him, with her stomach relaxed, there was still that nose—running, running, running. The knot in her stomach when her father was near with his interminable pressures was understandable, but the running nose? What in the world caused that?

When Millicent described her father she complained: "He's so *transparent,* and it's awful to see what's there. I want him to go away, as far from me as possible."

Later, as she confronted her running-nose symptom, the following dialogue emerged:

MUCUS: I'm the mucus running in Millicent's nose. I'm constantly irritating. I'm clear, transparent liquid. I don't have much substance. I'm constantly running, tickling, and irritating.

NOSE: I'm cartilage and skin. I have clear, watery liquid pouring out and I need constant attention. There's no way Millicent can ignore me. I'm a nuisance. I run all the time and I won't leave her alone. I'm inconsiderate and not concerned about anyone but myself. I come and go as I please. I interrupt Millicent's daily routine unexpectedly, without concern for her.

At this point, when Millicent heard her own words she exclaimed: "Like someone I know! That's my father! That's what he does at work—comes in and disrupts and absolutely drives me nuts. He's totally self-centered and not aware of anyone else around!"

Even though from the outside you might readily see the connection between Millicent's annoying transparent father and her disturbing transparent mucus, she herself did not know she had used the same word to describe both, and the resemblance came as a startling revelation to her. As yours will come to you, also, if you follow the procedure of giving words to the body parts related to *your* symptoms.

To go on with Millicent's running nose, which has more to teach us about the psycho-fundamentals of symptoms. At one point

Millicent was talking about how difficult her father was "because he never responds to me but goes off in his own distorted sense of reality." Then in an offhand way she said, "My father is crazy." When she uttered that casual phrase, she suddenly did a double-take. "Oh, my God!" she exclaimed, and then cried out, "I don't want him to be crazy!"

How we run from the reality of our parents' imperfections! And how securely we attempt to hide our feelings about those imperfections. And how painful are the revelations once they are uncovered. And how *necessary* in order to know ourselves.

Millicent had to learn that it was all right to have such feelings. If she felt that her father acted crazy, it didn't do him or her any good for her to go on concealing that feeling from herself.

When Millicent suffered the pain of the connection with the craziness of her father, she no longer had to run from that knowledge, and her nose decreased its running too.

Your symptoms—whatever they are—may camouflage painful yet necessary connections also, and it would be worth your while to address them using the format of Millicent's running nose.

Since the curative voice of your Inner Therapist speaks to you through your body's symptoms, you can apply the device of tuning in to a wide variety of bodily symptoms ranging from teeth-grinding and headache to constipation.

As we've seen over and over again, an effective way to begin listening to the voice of the Inner Therapist within the symptom is to start with a description of what is happening in that body part *from the point of view of the part itself.* While this device is applicable to everyone, each person will derive specific messages from it that relate to her or his individual life.

I've observed painful and persistent headaches clear up when the pains of conflict with one's mother were uncovered. And I've seen how chronic constipation—the holding on to feces and not letting them go—represented a holding on to mothers who were tenuous in their mothering, while the constipated persons disguised their forbidden rages against those unmothering mothers.

If you are suffering from asthma and begin to listen to the message in your symptom, you might learn that it is a way of smothering your rages instead of *realizing* them.

And people who grind their teeth are often found to swallow their resentments and be prone to martyr themselves even to their abusers—maybe *especially* to their abusers. Teeth grinders are often people who are kind to everyone except their own teeth, which they literally grind down mercilessly every night.

Are you plagued with eating disorders? Does your food addiction lead to a fat body? The fat symptom itself is created for important purposes and needs listening to. In one person's case (see my book *Fat Chance*) whose personality was self-effacing, her fat said: "I am large, important. I take up space. I demand attention." In another's, the fat was a symbolic assault on her mother: "My fat proves my mother was a bad mother and did nothing right. I get back at her." In another's it was a defense against parental assault. In another passive, amorphous-feeling person, her fat gave her definition: "My fat defines me." Mixtures of all of these can exist in the same person.

The fat body has a voice and gives volumes of messages that need heeding. The fat is a remarkable attention-getter—waiting, waiting to be heeded, not assaulted. If it is not heeded, if it is attacked with starvation diets and the like, it may slink off, only to come back again with fuller force as the 98 percent failure rate of almost all diet regimes indicates.

On the other side of the same coin are the people with anorexia, who have phobias about weight gain and stomach bulge. They are often in a state of war against the eternal female. You might say that these skinny bodies (usually but not always female) are in a power death-struggle with their mothers, whom they have incorporated inside themselves. Thus they go to life-threatening extremes to exorcise that "enemy." These living skeletons demand their starvation rites even to the brink of death, in order to gain control of that dominant female in their lives. Their bodies need listening to. Force-feeding only defeats the person cowering within, making her more desperate.

If you are suffering from an eating disorder, of whatever kind, consider what sort of body you have produced, and let that body talk to you and reveal your own secrets to your ears. That is the first step necessary to release your camouflaging energies to serve your inner growth.

Chronic facial expressions can also be considered symptoms. It is no accident that some people wear perennial smiles, others persistent frowns, still others ingenuous arched-eyebrow looks of constant surprise. Whatever your customary facial expression, it is there speaking loudly and clearly to all who look at you. It's now time for you to look at the expression yourself and to ask what message your internal healer-nurse-whole-maker is trying to reveal to you through your customary facial expression.

All these bodily manifestations are potential epiphanies for you. They can reveal truths necessary for healing yourself, for making you whole. They must be attended to. They are reminders, awakeners, promisers, gift-givers.

Your symptoms are important. Don't mask them with some ready-made medication. Don't assault them or cut them away. They are your creations. They are your direct lines of communication to your Inner Therapist, who wants to heal you, cure you, make you whole. It is your job to listen and to take care.

6
Feeling,
Nothing More Than Feeling

Music is feeling, then, not sound.
—*Wallace Stevens,*
"Peter Quince at the Clavier"

I feel, therefore I am.
—*Author*

Depression is easier to cope with than brain damage.
—*Jeanne Lindsay,*
in a personal communication

It is the property of all living creatures to *feel* pleasure or pain in a greater or less degree. All creatures which have life have feelings.
—*Crabb's English Synonyms*

At the end of December 1982, the radio blared with the news that *Time* magazine, which every year selects a Man of the Year, had for 1983 selected not a person but a *computer!* That tells it all.

Emotions continue to get very bad press. Let's take the emotion of elation or excitement, for example—and let's take it quickly, before it too yields to the computers and the pharmacological victors on the battlefield who would have us bland and comfortable at all cost.

Professional actors and actresses know that the excitement they feel prior to curtain time—commonly designated "stage fright"—adds a heightened electrical touch to their performances. Also performers in the other arts—musicians, opera singers, dancers, orators—know this phenomenon well. Many come to expect it and *use* the energy to enhance their performance. Some instead take a drug before performing.

Stage "fright" is really the adrenaline shooting through the body giving the energy for the anticipated task. The body's mechanism—the outpouring of adrenaline causing excitement, rapid heartbeat, supercharge of energy—is the same as in any fear-provoking situation, giving the energy for fight or flight, a normal and protective response to stress. In the case of the seasoned performer, the fright phenomenon is *welcome,* as long as it is within bounds and does not flood the organism and paralyze it. It is also a welcome development for others, because it provides the *force* to do great deeds—a mother with sudden incredible strength to lift an automobile off a stricken child, an energy to run beyond one's capacity in an emergency or under attack. The emergency, the crisis, evokes forces and substances in the body that are necessary for the extraordinary task required.

On the other hand, an actor without any preliminary excitement—a tranquilized performer—stepping out on stage is apt to lull the audience into a dullness. No one's adrenals are called upon to flow. The dullness is contagious, the lulling of the adrenals becomes an epidemic, and the audience yawns, falls asleep.

Thanks to the adrenal excitement felt by the creative artist and by contagion transmitted to the audience, everyone's adrenals keep flowing and the audience remains awake, alert, involved.

While most of us are not professional performers, we are all called upon to perform tasks in the daily art of living our lives, tasks we perform with varying degrees of aliveness or numbness. A mother giving "dull" time in extended hours to her child does more harm than a working mother who gives limited but excited "prime" time to her child. In terms of feelings, mere quantity of hours spent unfeelingly with a child are but multiples of zero and provide zero nourishment to the child.

Quality time is heartfelt and adrenalized, and nourishes profoundly.

I remember Anne, a mother with phobias of leaving her home. She was so guilty about never going out with her eight-year-old son that she compensated by playing endless games of checkers with him, a game she detested. With half a heart she tolerated the time spent with her son, while feeding him her camouflaged impatience and detestation. These are what he got from the hours she "sacrificed" for him.

On the other hand, Anne loved card games. I suggested she tell her son outright she didn't like to play checkers. After much reluctance she confessed to him. Much to her surprise, he was not devastated. Her dislike of checkers had been no secret to him, and he was relieved. Now they could play card games, which they both enjoyed, and she could feed him her involvement, enjoyment, and excitement, which nourished him and his own pleasure.

Simple? Yes, like most things in the good life.

We tend to be so distrustful of the simple things. We tend, too, to distrust our feelings, which cry out for our respect and attention.

When our feelings haven't been trained to fit a standardized or tranquilized mold, they often come unbidden from a deep life source within us. As with our dreams, if we persist in *not* paying attention to our feelings, they tend to stay out of sight, out of touch, and we are left to follow the false gods of programmed attitudes that merely pass for feelings, while we anxiously avoid those stirrings from within.

One of the most common feelings that "good" children and adults avoid, especially toward their parents, is in the category of anger, rage, and hate—the so-called negative emotions. Some people go so far as to cover up moderate resentments or even mild annoyances, while they spend their energy in dutiful and acquiescent behavior.

Another feeling relegated to the category of negative emotions is sadness with associated tears. When the sky cries and rains down we do things—we stay indoors, carry umbrellas, wear boots, even play in the rain. We take it in our stride. We know it's part of a natural balance that is taking place: low humidity, evaporation, increasing saturation, rain, low humidity. We'd be considered crazy if we thought the *sky* was sick when it was merely performing its natural balancing function when it rained.

But when people cry, especially women or children, they're told to *stop crying*—push the tears back, push the rain back, be sunny, smile. And when the crying persists, they're sent to psychiatrists who give them mood elevators (push the rain back) or electroshock (electrocute, explode the sky and make it, once and for all, stop raining).

All right, I hear you. And you're right. When the symptom goes too far, it does become unbearable. And something must be done. But the worst thing we can do is stifle the *voice* of the symptom. We need, above all, to hear its message.

Long ago I came to understand that people suffering from depression could be helped more readily if we changed the diagnosis from "depression" to "oppression." This semantic flipover did wonders for

79

my "depressed" patients. Instead of looking inside them for the *cause* of their illness— that is, instead of blaming them for being depressed—we examined and found the factors outside them (in their life, family, and work relationships) that were oppressive and causing despair.

If you look at depressed persons with their shoulders bowed forward, their chests caved in, their heads slung down, they really do give the impression that someone is standing over them with a whip. Hence, *oppression.*

I remember a young woman who dragged into my office weak, meek, pale, submissive, oppressed by a bombastic husband who wouldn't let her *breathe.* She couldn't have her own thoughts, activities, interests. Her life had to be for him, to serve only his wishes. He wouldn't have been able to get away with this domination of her had not her mother already indoctrinated her into being submissive. In a sense, she married her mother in the form of her tyrannical husband. She never peeped a peep of complaint against either of them. Instead, she got depressed. It was the only way she knew—the only way she could allow herself to be.

When I lent support to her peeps of dissent, this downtrodden, depressed lamb being led to slaughter became a raging tigress toward her oppressors—in my office, that is. And her depression, which had been tinged with ideas of suicide, lifted. I'll never forget the rage that came out of that theretofore lifeless lump and how it transformed her life. And she never had to let her oppressors *hear* her rage. It was important that *she* herself heard it.

All right, back to you, waiting with your depression/oppression for some relief. You can start with a simple exercise: Think of all the factors—people, situations, things—in your life that in one way or another oppress you. Ah, ah—I hear some of you saying you have no oppressions and that everybody is so kind to you and they all wish you well.

Yes, yes—they can all wish you well, intend for you to be well, and still *feel* oppressive to you. It is not their *intentions* you must address, but *your feelings* when you think of them, when you're with them. It may not be as obvious, perhaps, as a slave driver cracking the whip on your bare back. Nothing so obvious perhaps. In fact, the more subtle it is—the more good those significant others *intend* for your welfare and the more they *love* you—the more oppressive they can be.

So don't be beguiled by their declarations or good intentions. Remember the proverb. The road to hell is paved with them. The road to *your* living hell is paved with *their* good intentions toward you. It is those very good intentions that give those significant others the thought that they have the *right* to dictate to you, to dominate you. After all, it's for your good, isn't it? Don't they want the best for you?

So—we are not here analyzing the people or things that oppress you, or their intentions. We are rather attempting to discern *your own actual feelings*. That's all—just *your feelings*.

And right now, for our beginning dig into the field of your depression, we start by excavating any shoot or root or pebble of a feeling of oppression that may be there. Leave no stone unturned in your search. If *feeling of oppression* is too strong a concept for you to admit to, see if you have some lighter feelings—say, little laments, even a tiny whine in you about some real or even imagined slight. That's just the point. It doesn't even have to be a real slight. Even a slight you *imagine* may be there because of the feeling of having been slighted. A mere wisp of a feeling will do if there is no outright hurt.

Here I want to make something clear. I'm not suggesting that as soon as you find the hidden resentment, rage, or anger that you go immediately to the persons and dump it all on them. No, this is not an exercise *against them*. It's *for you*. For your own awareness and understanding. For your own liberation. Not for you to become in turn the oppressor to your oppressors. Fritz Perls, author of *Gestalt Therapy Verbatim,* as did many others, understood depression to be rage turned inward (unexpressed rage). Dr. Perls held that the way to get over your own depression was to make someone else depressed. While as a symptom-relieving technique this does work, we are after fullness, not revenge—not spreading the misery, not getting rid of our symptoms at the expense of another.

So, this may reassure the fainthearted lambs among you that I don't intend for you to become the raging lioness I described earlier. I intend only for you to be aware of a reality of your very own that you have buried, and of how you've used your depressive symptoms to help the burial so very neatly and securely. Here again we see how we are plagued with dichotomies, being as we are the animal par excellence of the eternal paradox. *The best disguise is to act opposite to our reality. And the best disguise for raging anger is docile depressiveness.* In fact, the disguise works so well that even the persons themselves don't know what lurks underneath their masks of depression.

With this introduction, perhaps you are now ready to resume the first task: Step One—List each time you've been angry or resentful or felt slighted. You can start with the people in your life today and your experiences with them.

As you list each person, write a short or long statement describing the incident that evoked that feeling in you.

If you're really in bad shape, very severely "depressed," you probably feel that *you* are to blame for everything, that you are so horrible you don't even deserve any decent attention or treatment from anybody, that in fact you're like a devil incarnate and all the rest of the people around you are angels. This is common in so-called depression. What this kind of thinking indicates is that the resentment is very deeply buried and very deeply disguised and will take a lot of doing—heavy dredging, a derrick at the least—to get to it.

There are several ways we can approach this problem, since we know that anger is an emotion all people not only are capable of (remember the adrenal glands and their outpouring of raging adrenalin) but also *feel* on some level. And if it isn't permitted to be felt on an *emotional* level, it will be converted and felt on a *physical* level.

For instance, Constance loved her mother but also had feelings of another sort toward her, feelings which Constance never permitted herself to *know*. She was mortally afraid of causing her mother any hurt or pain, and her mother played on this and always got her own way with Constance. Constance's mother was very competitive with her and subtly always found ways to put her down and then climb on top.

Constance had a compulsion to get involved with married men, until one day she made the connection: "That's one time my mother can't take the men away from me. They're already married." She became aware of her feeling that her mother took everything else away from her, and if she had a relationship with a single man, she always lost him to her mother.

Notwithstanding all of this, whenever Constance's anger began to surface, with the tiniest tinge of it as in the form of a mild complaint, her mother would begin to cry and Constance's anger would get mortared over. The only sign remaining would be in the form of a somatic symptom—pain in the back between her shoulder blades (where her mother was symbolically knifing her?) and headaches. Whenever there was any danger of her angry feelings coming through, and her angry feelings meant that her mother would be hurt and also angry at her (and maybe on some deeper level she was afraid her mother might kill her)—whenever Constance's angry feelings threatened to emerge, she would, instead, get a headache or an ache in her upper back.

Constance did not allow herself to *feel* her anger against her mother until she was somehow assured that her feeling this would not hurt her mother. And once Constance permitted herself to *feel* her own complaints, resentments, angers, she no longer needed to mortar them up in her back and head, and the pains in both places disappeared.

Back to *you*. If you tend to deny your feelings of resentment, especially toward the people you love and whom you want to love you and approve of you, then you'll have to work overtime to uncover those forbidden or denied feelings.

If you can somehow accept the assurance that the ambivalent, inevitably uncertain human being is *always* a mixture of light and dark, opposing feelings, contradictory thoughts and ideas in constant tugs of war, then you would know that resentment is not only permissible toward those we love but essential. Resentment is tied to its opposite state—acceptance—in as intimate and inevitable a connection-continuum as night is tied to day.

If you readily can muster up feelings of resentment or even rage against others, if you've never had any difficulty doing this, you probably can't imagine why it would be necessary for me to be insisting how natural a phenomenon is the eruption of anger or resentment for us adrenalized anxious human beings. But the vast numbers of you who would apologize for someone's bumping into you would know instantly how difficult it is not only to express the anger but even to permit yourself to *feel* it in the first place.

More and more, the psychiatric divisions of hospitals are filling with people who are overcome with massive guilt for harboring the slightest tinges of resentment. Clearly, these people are crying out *not* for the punitive electrocution of their brain cells but for the *permission* to feel their resentment, for the permission to harbor their dark or vengeful thoughts which testify not to their beastliness but to their human state.

If you belong to this category of anger-suppressed persons, I would urge you especially to attend to the tasks I've set forth and to start by listing the people who have caused anything from annoyance to rage for anything from a slight stepping on your toe to a storm-trooping on your heart. When this list and description of each incident is completed, with much attention paid to specific detail not only of their offense but of your reaction, then you are ready for Step Two.

Step Two—Out of Depression. This step is particularly aimed at those of you who have had trouble accepting your resentful feelings. You are to go over each item in the list you've just made and imagine the offense against you *magnified*. Picture it as considerably worse than it was in actuality, exaggerate it out of all proportion. So, for example, if it was a teacher who criticized you unjustly, picture that teacher screaming at you, denouncing you and humiliating you in front of the class. If it was your mother who angered you by not letting you stay out as late as you wished, picture her getting more restrictive and not letting you go out at all. If a boss reprimanded you for being late or absent, picture him or her firing you. If a spouse or a friend kept you waiting, picture her or him coming even later, or leaving you stranded and not showing up at all. Exaggerate the time—see yourself waiting for a whole day, or several, or waiting at a wedding ceremony for your bride or groom who never shows. Build up the drama to melodramatic dimensions. Fantasize a wild melodrama, exaggerated, caricatured, until you *feel the blame going outward,* the resentment rising, the anger flowing. When you can achieve this, you are well on the way to changing the tides of your depression.

If you are unable to feel the outward-bound blame, if you insist that any abuse from others is all your own fault, then you must fancifully exaggerate that abuse even more. Use the most outrageous flights of your imagination to picture your abusers. Make their oppression or contempt or humiliation of you even more severe. Grow horns on their heads if need be; make them devilish, tormenting. Fantasize anything you need to in order to get your blame going *away* from yourself and *toward* the others.

Some people seem to do this quite naturally; they are always blaming others for everything. Take lessons from them on how it is done. These blaming types are often the very ones who create around them oppressed/depressed people whom they can blame and make more depressed.

Be unfair, unjust—anything you have to be to get your imagination working and your depression lifting. Remember, you're not hurting anybody else, no matter what you fantasize, and you're helping yourself.

And now, Step Three—Turning the Tables. This should not be attempted until you've gotten the blame and then the anger flowing outward. Continue with Step Two no matter how long it takes, exercising your imagination until you can successfully picture out-and-out abuse of yourself and until you feel some blame toward the offending parties. Then turn the tables on your oppressors.

Never fear, those people you picture treating as they have treated you will still be prancing around trying to dominate you or put you down as has been their custom. Your fantasy is designed not actually to hurt them but to *liberate* you—to liberate you to the human condition of eye for eye, tooth for tooth tendency that we've been part of for thousands of years. So, welcome your fantasy to the human race and let the avalanche proceed.

Again I want to make it clear that this exercise is not meant for you to go knock somebody's block off. It's effective without that. The *awareness* of your anger is the essential step here. That's the beauty of it. You don't have to get violent in order to free yourself of the violence and abuse from others. You can awaken from your depression merely by admitting that the violence in feeling or thought exists in you and is permissible in you. It does not make you a monster—it makes you a human being like everyone else.

Now, if you've carried out these simple steps and gone to a wild extreme of unreasonable destructiveness in your fantasies, and if you allow the extreme to get so extreme that it begins to tickle your funny bone, and if you somehow begin to chuckle, then you know you've gone through the depression/oppression to the other side. It's a sign that you're beginning to let go of your grip on the depressive symptoms. The chuckle or outright laugh is like the raging fever breaking—it augurs the decline of the sickness, the end of the crisis, the beginning of a healthy process.

Your Inner Therapist would have been able to tell you all these steps to follow, but sometimes we're so out of it, so mired in symptoms, that we keep the therapeutic voice out of earshot.

Remember, with depression/oppression as with any other symptom or syndrome, the first step is to describe *what is*. The second step is to determine what function it serves, who is helped by it, who is hindered by it, what effects it causes.

The third step is to determine how those functions, those effects, those helpings and hindrances can be achieved in any other, perhaps more direct, manner.

And the fourth step is to picture this achievement in a series of trial-and-error mental test runs before any overt action is taken.

Since most of us tend to kid ourselves one way or another every step of the way of our lives, the use of the Inner Therapist as an *objective consultant* is of inordinate help. We can recognize its voice when it deals with *survival needs*. When a voice talks about *wants, wishes, happiness,* and the like, then we can be certain it is our *subjective* voice or old tapes of early authority figures from our past who frequently are false guides to pseudo fulfillment.

In step one—the actual situation: if you are a committed non-blamer, you would be likely to say that everyone around you is fine and dandy. But if you asked your Inner Therapist to tell you who is unfair, unjust, disapproving, ungiving, ungenerous, judgmental, and so on, your Inner Therapist, sitting there projected before you, would most likely come up with one somebody at the very least. And then the dialogue can ensue, with your asking your Inner Therapist what that somebody does to you. You can ask your Inner Therapist to help you describe the incident and then to help with describing your *feelings* in response to the somebody's deeds, and on and on. Soon you begin to have a real therapeutic interchange with an objective guide to lead you through the three steps I've indicated earlier.

7
Am I
My Neighbor's Keeper?

A man should learn to detect and watch that gleam of light which flashes across his mind from within, more than the lustre of the firmament of bards and sages. Yet he dismisses without notice his thought, because it is his. In every work of genius we recognize our own rejected thoughts: they come back to us with a certain alienated majesty.　　—*Ralph Waldo Emerson, "Self-Reliance"*

The flowers appear on the earth;
The time of the singing of birds is come,
And the voice of the turtle is heard in our land.
　　—*Song of Solomon 2:12*

Illnesses are people, people and their ways of life; and so we're getting rid of people when we get rid of their alleged illnesses.
　　—*Peter Breggin, M.D.,*
The Crazy from the Sane

And the voice of the symptom shall be heard in the land when our spring arrives.

Although the Inner Therapist speaks to us most eloquently through our symptoms, it has other voices too. One of these is not quite a voice but a whisper across the inner ear. We hear these whispers from time to time—and our typical response is to ignore them, to let them be wafted away.

Sometimes the message comes as an image that flashes momentarily in the mind, and we tend to push this too into the dark shadows.

I'm not referring to an esoteric experience relegated to a select few artistic types or to the inspired or mad persons who hear voices or have hallucinations. The experience can be as ordinary as buying a car from a used-car salesperson in which transaction the critical question, on which your purchase depends, vibrates for a split second in your mind. Instead of stopping to connect with that vibration, you go on following the salesperson's thread intended of course to sell the car. Once you toss away the whispered question— let's say, for example, it is something like: "What about the service record of the car?" or "Is the car the original owner's?"—once you toss this away, the question generally doesn't occur to you again until *after* you've plunked your money down and driven away and run into mechanical difficulties. Then you remember the whisper in the ear which you let drift off.

Or it can be not banal but an important life-or-death thought that flashes like a meteor across the firmament of your mind—for example, a question to a doctor like: "What are the adverse side effects of this medication you are prescribing?" Or a question to a surgeon like: "What would happen if I don't have the operation?" Or the 64-dollar question to any doctor which tests her or his mettle: "What if I get a consultation for another opinion?" (Since no one person can possibly have all the answers, this last is a perfectly reasonable and self-protective question, though admittedly it is not designed to ingratiate you with doctors who have weak egos.)

It is essential that we start listening to our body's wisdom, to our inner protective voices. We must learn to see the inner flashes, to hear the whisperings in our inner ears.

George Santayana warned:

> It is not wisdom to be only wise,
> And on the inward vision close the eyes.

Our greatest danger is our failure to heed the voice within, the vision within, while we defer to external authorities.

Since this is not the best of all possible worlds, and we do not come from perfect families, we are left carrying in our psyches the marks of those imperfections. Yet in a paradoxical way common to the human psyche, the very imperfections are themselves a means of reaching toward that perfection for which we yearn.

How we long for paradise. Each psychological aberration manifests that longing. Every mental quirk is designed to balance that very quirk, to set things right, to arrive at a state of grace—total acceptance and pure love.

Typically our behavior belies our intent. Often those with the greatest longing for human contact and warmth appear the most contemptuous. Those who run from party to party, from person to person, are often the most isolated and lonely. Those who appear the most aggressive and independent often long to be taken care of. It is because of this confusion and contradiction between longing (intent) and behavior (psychological state) that we lose the gift of being able to see ourselves as others see us.

First we adjust our mask, and then we look in the mirror. We cover that mask with another, and then we let the neighbors see. Always we are on stage, and the audience is composed of critics. We play the roles we have been trained to play for some deep balancing need of our imperfect parents, who strive to perfect themselves, correct their defects, while imprinting their unfulfilled needs on us. Forever we play the designated roles designed to gratify *their needs* while busily deluding ourselves in our belief of how independent of them we are, how different. We *think* we are free, self-motivated, while at heart we cringe with the sense of our abjectness. Our hearts know who pulls our strings.

What to do? What to do?

How can we come to know the self behind the mask behind the mask?

Is anybody home?

Or is there but another mask, and another, and another, to deny and defend? And still another . . . and another.

Is there a self to know? And why should we want to know more, when what we already know gives such trouble? Ah, such confusion.

The worst way to deal with our confusion is to *deny* its presence and assume that our ready-made disguises are our substance rather than our cover-up.

What is your most obvious psychological disguise—the one your neighbors see and most know about? What is the trait you display most prominently to the world?

Each society fosters particular traits through subtle reward and punishment systems.

Thus, in a competitive society of Horatio Algers and the-sky's-the-limit, survival-of-the-fittest and the-devil-take-the-hindmost attitudes are acceptable. So it should not be surprising that there abound such states as suspiciousness, distrust, paranoia (suspiciousness and distrust in their extreme degree), and competitiveness; and the related states of jealousy, isolation, and loneliness.

If I am not my brother's or sister's or neighbor's keeper in a cooperative, responsible, sharing sense, if my neighbor is not myself but someone out to try to climb on top of me, then it's a setup for me to try to combat those neighbors' attempts by getting on top first. Pushing out of economic necessity to be among the first in line is a setup that would be hard for even the most altruistic, congenial personalities to resist. How can we be the keeper of our neighbors when they are out to slit our economic throats because of their own needs?

From this point of view, it becomes impossible to approach the psychological state of any human being—or the state of any other living creature for that matter—in a vacuum without regard to the surrounding influences and exigencies. Remember, we are the adaptational animal par excellence. We are our culture.

For every person who by some fluke or strange mutation is free to know that "all human beings are made of each other" (Peter Breggin, M.D., *The Crazy from the Sane;* Lyle Stuart, 1971) there are swarms of others to perpetuate the same old competitive traits.

You there, with your psychological quirks fully upon you—are you suspicious, distrustful? What does it matter to you where it comes from, your condition, or who or what caused it? You've got it, and it interferes with your well-being, and that's what you're concerned with. But it seems futile to think of changing it. If you let your guard down, they'll get you, knock *you* down, get on top. There's no rest for your weary bones—you'll always have to be on the lookout, watchful—watching what you say, how you say it, whom you say it to, who overhears you. Do the clicks on your phone mean it's bugged—someone's spying on you? Are the people at work watching you while you're watching them while pretending not to be watching them at all while they're pretending not to be watching you . . . while you . . . while they . . . you . . . they . . . you . . .

Help! You're in a labyrinth, caught in a maze, everyone's eyes upon you, upon your every movement, your every twitch. You dress the way you're supposed to dress for the occasion, talk the way you're supposed to talk (maybe they won't see you if you dress and act like all the others, you who so much want to be noticed) . . . and in the meantime you're so busy watching *them* you call their attention to yourself. Your eyes, on them, have no time for even a sneak glance at yourself, and certainly no time for an inward look.

Gone is the smallest semblance of an inward vision. You have eyes only for *them*. You have a new occupation: master spy. And when you've finally achieved this distinction, spying out all those eyes on you, you have crossed over the barrier and entered the realm of the *pure paranoid*.

But don't worry. You're not alone. You have loads of company . . . all around . . . *everywhere!*

What can you do, if you're waiting, with your guard up, watching lest your neighbor (or somebody's neighbor—aren't all people by extension your neighbor?) take your job or rob your home when you go out to work? Here you are with your paranoia a built-in fixture in your life. On guard! Ha! they didn't foil you—you were watching all the time. They didn't catch you by surprise.

To be paranoid is to expect from others what we would do unto them—though secretly, to be sure. So very secret is that which we would do unto others that it's hidden from ourselves most of all, tucked neatly into our unconscious.

If this view of paranoia is correct—and it is generally accepted that what we fear most from others is the very thing we find most unacceptable in ourselves and therefore *must* continue to project that abhorrent thing onto others, blaming them for what we refuse to face within—if this view of paranoia reflects the actual state of affairs, and if it applies also to lesser forms of paranoia such as suspiciousness, distrust, excessive jealousy, then the way to deal with the problem is clear.

Remembering that it is the hidden, shameful thing within you whose presence you most deny and which you are most likely to fear from others (mostly because you've projected that outward and thus alleviated the shame and guilt of harboring such an "undesirable" trait or tendency), we have our clue as to the first step you must take if you want to clear up that disturbing entity. And that step is *inward*.

Do you wake up some morning and suddenly feel suspicious that your spouse is philandering, even though he or she has been totally submerged in the family, has spent every evening at home with you, has been a loyal and faithful companion, has never wandered off the beaten track? And does your suspicion become more and more intensified, so that you are overcome with it and begin to accuse your partner more and more until your accusations become incessant and you begin to tell everyone of how your partner in life is deceiving you? And do you tell *everyone* about it—your children,

91

your neighbors, even strangers on the street in extreme cases?

Or are you the kind of man who feels very threatened at the thought of your wife's going out to work—out there where you don't know whom she'll be talking to or looking at, where you won't know where she is every minute once she's out of the safe niche of the house you provided for her? Does your daughter's going out on dates set you in a frenzy if she returns after 11 P.M.—or 10 P.M.?

Are you the kind of parent who goes berserk with distrustfulness if your teen-aged children go out with friends and return after midnight?

Suspiciousness and distrust often erode the very relationships they are trying to protect.

You there, with whatever the sources of your suspiciousness, if you can stand the anxiety of confronting the underlying shames within yourself, you have an opportunity to use those unbidden tensions of your suspiciousness in a constructive way for yourself and for your relationships with your loved ones.

If you want to deal with this, if those feelings of distrust are threatening to overwhelm you, then the next time you feel the suspiciousness rising, you might say to yourself: "I am going to work on this." Once the decision is made, go to a room where there are no distractions and no interruptions (free of telephone, TV, radio, door bell). *Get yourself in a comfortable position and take a few slow, deep breaths.* In the course of this exercise, should tensions begin to rise, you can stop and take those deep breaths again—take as many as you like or need in order to get in touch with yourself. If the breaths are *slow* and *deep,* you can control the hyperventilation-anxiety cycle. (People can bring on an anxiety attack by hyperventilating—rapid shallow breathing. Conversely, they can stop a hyperventilating anxiety attack instantly simply by slowing and deepening their breathing.)

When you are relaxed you can start the exercise: *Bring to mind the fantasy—the one that plagues you—in which your distrust or suspiciousness begins to get out of bounds.* If you allow yourself to visualize your worst fears in fantasy, you will be less likely to provoke into being the very thing you fear most. Keep in mind as you are doing this fantasy that this is *your* fantasy of those distrusted, suspected others, just as your suspiciousness is *your* state.

This exercise is designed to familiarize you with what is *yours,* in you. It is not designed to deny any possible external reality, nor to validate it. Your Inner Therapist creates these psychological states of mind, these symptoms, for *your* edification. They need attending to—not by rushing off in a volatile accusatory escapade but by your going in, to hear out in full the message of that internal therapeutic voice. It is there to teach you how to fulfill your life. Therefore you would do well, in that solitary room, to give your fantasy free rein and let it complete itself, no matter how distressing it may be for the moment. An underlying greater distress is readying itself to be attended to, to be relieved, in the process. You are readying yourself to learn not about that other person out there on whom you focused your suspicions, but about yourself.

I cannot tell you what you will learn in that room when you allow yourself to visualize your suspicions to their fullest. Nor can I tell what you will learn if you refuse the task, refuse to go beyond the first dim inkling that you are being betrayed by that significant other. Each person's story and discovery takes place in a unique fashion, even though the underlying themes may be universal. There's a credulous Othello waiting to be inflamed into suspiciousness in just about all of us.

Let's look at what others learned when they approached their psychological states as symptoms containing therapeutic messages from their Inner Therapist.

Mrs. Noble was known by her neighbors as a hardworking, diligent housewife and mother of four lusty children. Her husband, also industrious, worked long hours as a cabinetmaker to support his growing family and send the children to college. Like his wife, he was family-oriented.

When her youngest child was a senior in high school, Mrs. Noble began to have suspicions that her husband was running around with other women. Her suspicions grew until she became openly accusatory. Her children's and husband's attempts to reassure her of his loyalty were to no avail. Her suspiciousness became so extreme that it threatened to grow into full-fledged paranoia. She began talking to strangers in supermarkets about her husband's infidelities, and at the same time believed that the neighbors were out to steal her husband from her. People began to say she was off her rocker.

In a lucid interval Mrs. Noble allowed herself to face the fantasy that was destroying her relationship with her husband and children, the very people she loved most in the world. With great difficulty, resistance, and anxiety she permitted herself to visualize the entire scenario—Mr. Noble having sex with an unidentified woman, maybe a neighbor, a client, a stranger. The scenario, allowed to come to completion in her fantasy, ends of course with his falling in love with one or several women and deciding to leave home. This climax had never been permitted previously.

This was not the full climax of her scenario, but rather a mini-climax, a prelude to the real thing. The scenario, continued to its full conclusion in her fantasy, showed Mrs. Noble alone—alone and unloved, her husband and children gone. That was the worst of it, her aloneness. Projecting her wish to cling to relationships onto her husband and his women helped Mrs. Noble cover her panic of her children's separations, her menopausal condition in which her youth was separating from her, and now her youngest child readying to leave her with an empty nest.

A simplified view of projection would have stated that Mrs. Noble wanted to have the forbidden sexual affairs she accused her husband of having but would not have touched the intenser problems of living her life. *It was relationships with loved ones and with herself,* confronting the realities of her life's conditions, that were needed.

And once she lighted on the underlying threat of aging and encroaching loneliness of a woman who had spent her adult life serving others, who had not developed any non-family-related skills or interests, her suspicions lifted as a dark veil.

Or take the case of Tony B., a father with jealous rages. Jealousy, the green-eyed monster, is a state of guarded possessiveness. We are jealous when we want to hold on to, dominate, and possess a person or thing and don't want anyone else to get it.

Tony, an affluent head of a large corporation, did not covet others' possessions. He was envious of no one. But he jealously guarded his own. He "owned" his wife and daughter and watched over them well. Tony had refused to allow his wife to work, insisting she be available for his needs, and she seemed content to comply. His daughter had spent a cloistered adolescence under Tony's watchful eye. But now, at nineteen, she was beginning to emerge. He was fearful that she was being "too free" when she wanted to go out to movies with friends. Occasionally, in a rage, he would strike her, once hurling a chair at her when she said she would go out even if he didn't like it.

At work Tony was well liked. He treated his employees with respect. His associates at his country club sought him out as a golf and dinner companion. They never dreamed he possessed such raging demons, for he was always so generous and courteous with them.

Whereas Tony espoused marital fidelity and premarital chastity for his wife and daughter, he did not himself adhere to these principles when he, discreetly, pursued assignations with other men's wives and daughters. "After all, I'm a man!" he declared, not sensing the contradiction.

When the conflict with his daughter became severe Tony allowed himself to go through the fierce anxiety of visualizing his daughter as the slut he feared she would turn into if he let her go out with friends. During this visualization he confronted two more fearful underlying themes in himself. One was the fear of loss of power and potency with the consequent feelings of helplessness and vulnerability. The other was the fear of people's ridicule. Both fears were wrapped within the green-tinged visions of his daughter's alleged lusts.

A more superficial view of Tony's excessive jealousy might remain stuck with the obvious explanation that he denied his wife's and daughter's freedoms because of his own sexual excesses. But Tony's symptoms needed more intense listening to, for his jealousy had become so excessive that he was in danger of alienating his wife and daughter altogether. Previously Tony had stopped the voice of his symptom through which spoke his Inner Therapist by violently acting out his jealous rages. Now, at the crossroad of a family crisis, he permitted himself to hear the underlying message from which he had earlier fled at such great cost to his own and his family's well-being. And he began to meet himself in a new way. This, in turn, enabled him to meet his wife and daughter in a more accepting and understanding way.

All psychological states can be dealt with using the same process of listening to the *whole story* that the Inner Therapist is trying to tell us through our psychological states and our symptoms.

Feelings of inferiority and worthlessness, low self-esteem, and placating behavior have a hidden design. We don't have to be stuck playing out the same old roles, allowing ourselves to be kicked by the world. We can get into that solitary room, play out the tapes, breathe, ready ourselves to meet our Inner Therapist and hear the underlying plan unfold, the plan on which is built the psychological state we find so undesirable.

The process of hearing the voice is the same for all: follow the story, the scenario, down to its excruciating conclusion and face, through your creative imagination, the *consequences* of that finale. There, in the consequences, is the heart of the matter. That heart, though pained, contains your Inner Therapist waiting to nurture you.

In the same way, states of superiority, grandiosity, and contemptuousness contain an underlying story, a lesson for you. You don't have to remain stuck in the role you have been trained to play, the attitude you've been indoctrinated to maintain. Change is waiting at your deepest human level.

Other psychological conditions that plague many people come in the form of obsessions (insistent thoughts that give us little space for other considerations) and compulsions (actions that seem to take over and control us).

The kinship between obsessions (such as food obsessions leading to obesity or anorexia) and addictions (such as alcoholism) is apparent in that the individuals are beset by thoughts, drives, and urges that produce enormous anxiety. We might say that people who are obsessed or addicted develop those states in order to deal with the anxiety that threatens to overwhelm them.

People with obsessions and addictions can be approached in much the same way as those with other psychological conditions—not by attacking or assaulting the symptom but by listening to its voice, suffering the anxiety that the messages evoke, learning that the anxiety isn't lethal (whereas the symptom carried to excess may be), and giving the anxious person space to expand.

In reference to food obsessions, the poet and essayist Randall Jarrell wisely said: "Inside every fat man there is a man who is starving. Part of you is being starved to death, and the rest of you is being stuffed to death" ("A Sad Heart at the Supermarket").

There are many ways in which we are starving—not only through addictions.

Anxiety or no, to listen to the starved inner self yearning to be fed the proper nurturance is our most vital task. Our Inner Therapist is there to aid us.

8
Love,
Where Are Your Eyes?

The archenemy of intimacy is conformity.
—Author

Cupid and my Campaspe play'd
At cards for kisses, Cupid paid. . . .
At last he set her both his eyes—
She won, and Cupid blind did rise.
O Love! has she done this to thee?
What shall, alas! become of me?
—John Lyly (1553–1606),
"Cupid and Campaspe"

The trouble with this wide-open pornography . . . is not that it . . .
unleashes the passions but that it cripples the emotions; not that it
encourages a mature attitude but that it is a reversion to infantile
obsessions. . . . Prowess is proclaimed but love is denied. What we
have is not liberation but dehumanization.
—Norman Cousins,
The Saturday Review, *September 20, 1975*

Love, love, where are your eyes?

Is that screeching hellion, threatening to gouge me of every last
cent I own, the demure soft-tongued girl I married?

Is that brutalizing monster, riding roughshod over me and my
dreams, the attentive gallant I wed?

Where has love fled?

Where were our eyes?

Divorces are rampant. Relationships fall off like flies. Families
are disintegrating.

The center will not hold.

97

Where is the remedy? And the remedy for *what*?

What is the *condition* we would remedy?

I've heard it said that the worst reason for marrying is love. Yet all worthwhile relationships are based on love to one degree or another—love between pupil and teacher, family members, lovers, friends, neighbors.

Love, being a blind god, has no eyes to look in judgment. Hence relationships, insofar as they are loving, are never judgmental. They are blind to size, shape, color, age, race, sex, and economic or mental status. They defy convention and conformity.

The ancient Greeks who made Cupid a young blind god thereby showed a wisdom that has much to teach us concerning loving relationships, starting with the relationship with the self. Relationships with others reflect the kind of relationship we have with ourselves.

If you look in the mirror full of accusatory eyes, eyes glaring in contempt at the fat thighs or bulging belly, eyes assessing the graying hair or sagging jowls, eyes measuring the oversized ears or short or tall of the stature, eyes disdaining the light or dark of the skin or hair or its texture—if you look upon yourself with this many-eyed judgment, there is no way you can emerge with any semblance of self-esteem or love. For after fixing and formulating yourself with these accusations, assessments, and measurements, there is no way Cupid's arrow can penetrate and liberate your relationship with yourself, nor therefore with *any other person*.

And yet, how can we get away from these measurings? We are obsessed with perfectionisms, with *ideal* weights and *ideal* noses. Are we not always reaching beyond our grasp?

Early in our lives our culture's, together with our specific family's, ideal is imprinted somewhere behind our eyes. And forever after we superimpose this image on everything we look at, measuring every form against the dimensions and qualities and characteristics of our "ideal image." Beauty *is* in the eyes (and the mind) of the beholder.

Many years ago I came across a James Thurber cartoon in which an exceedingly round butterball of a woman and an equally rotund man were sitting on a couch looking moony-eyed at each other. The caption read: *"The heart has reasons that the reason cannot know."*

Love is in the heart of the beholder. Love, blind, defies measurement. When someone looks at us with measuring eyes, when a parent or spouse insists that we have an operation on our nose or face to "correct" or improve upon nature (to flatten a bump or stretch out a wrinkle), and when we look at ourselves with measuring eyes, we—they—are unloving. This is the real conflict then—the unlovingness in the concern with measurements—and not whether the nose or face should be altered.

Love has been variously described, defined, explicated, complicated. Shakespeare, on loving relationships, considered that merely thinking of the loved person was replenishing: ". . . if the while I think on thee, dear friend, all losses are restored, and sorrows end." Goethe, more modestly, claimed that pain shared is halved and happiness shared is doubled. Ashley Montagu sees loving relationships as those which bestow creative enhancement on others.

Certainly when we know love at all, we know it as a flow, a flowing outward, a flowing from the loved source inward. We know most that we are *alive* when we most feel loving and loved. The flow glows. We feel well nourished.

It's a paradox in human relationships that repression of angry, hostile feelings stifles the flow of lovingness and that, conversely, allowing the angry, hostile feelings to come to full awareness takes the lid off the flow of warm, loving feelings. In fact, some mythologies have Cupid (Eros) as the son of Aphrodite and Ares (the Greek god of war!).

We've been brainwashed to think that honoring our mothers and fathers means we must not have angry feelings toward them, but this early brainwashing cripples all subsequent relationships. I remember a patient who was getting in touch with some hating feelings toward her husband after twenty-five years of marriage. She was horrified. "If I hate him, that means my whole life has been a lie!" she exclaimed. How hard it is for us to accept our own ambivalences!

How can we feel flowings of love when we stifle the flow of our other feelings, our ambivalences? How can we love others when we are so full of contempt for our own measurements, when we are so full of self-hatings, self-doubtings, self-recriminations? Our alienation from others starts with our separation from our selves. This is the rift that needs to be healed first before a bridge to and from others is built. And for this healing work our Inner Therapist is handsomely equipped.

Fifty-year-old Willa had had a dutiful but cold relationship with her mother all her life. She insisted that she loved her mother and that she was distressed only when her mother used her as a shield against her husband, whom her mother constantly belittled. Little Willa had been trained to take her mother's side against her father, and she never came to grips with her antagonisms toward her mother, who had prevented Willa from expressing the loving she felt for her father.

Willa later married a man whom she began to demean as her mother had demeaned her father, but toward whom Willa was very dutiful, as she had been toward her mother. Willa's husband, though passive, yet dominated Willa much as her mother had dominated her. Had Willa married her mother?

Gradually Willa's husband, whom she had subtly cast in a woman's role, became sexually malfunctioning. Clearly there had ceased to be any *flow* in that relationship.

It wasn't until Willa faced up to the coldness and dutifulness toward her mother that the flow of long since buried rages and hostilities began to pour out. These all but devastated her. How could she feel so hateful to her poor suffering mother, who was by now an ailing seventy-five-year-old?

But there was no stopping the flow once the floodgates were opened. Yet, once these hating feelings flushed out, Willa contacted feelings even more deeply buried—soft, warm, vibrant, glowing, nourishing, loving. It was the first time in fifty years that Willa expressed something other than duty toward her mother. And her mother—cantankerous, ailing, aging—glowed in responsiveness. They nourished each other.

And now Willa's husband could stop playing the role of mother-in-disguise and could regain his manhood with Willa.

Willa's story is not unique. It teaches us not only that the negative emotions do not destroy relationships but that those emotions need to be experienced. Else, we dish out and receive pseudo love—a cold nonnurturing platter at best.

The need to keep some connection with our primary nurturer is fundamental, and to maintain that connection we do all manner of things in the expectation that the nurturer—mostly mother—will love us. How we seek love! How we *need* it! We even build huge, burdensome bodies for the sake of connecting links.

When Kate was thirteen, her mother put her head in an oven and turned the gas on. The gas blew the glass out of the kitchen windows and Kate's mother's life was saved.

Kate subsequently built a kitchen-related body to keep some connection with the depressed suicidal mother whom she consciously hated. In this respect, this overt hating, she differed from Willa, whose hating was submerged.

What was submerged in Kate? What was she hiding? Consciously she despised her mother, who had stayed in bed instead of nurturing Kate during her needy childhood. Kate decidedly had no problem with the negative emotions. And yet Kate needed nurturance. So she found a symbolic way of connecting with her malnurturer—the construction of an enormously fat body. It was easier than to feel the pain of deprivations, the pain of frustrated longings and lovings that had for so many of her formative years gone unrequited. The pains of her unrequited loving needed to be unconcealed, experienced, allowed to flow.

Twenty-seven-year-old Dee, another food-obsessed woman, carried an extra hundred pounds of weight. Her "skinny" mom was very critical. Dee's mom had always been attentive to Dee's father to the exclusion of Dee, going on trips with him and never going to school for class night meetings with Dee's teachers nor to see any of Dee's school performances.

When Dee asked herself what she would risk by losing her fat, she said: "I'd lose a bridge to my mother and to my mother's attention."

Despite this insight, Dee declared: "No matter what weight I am, I'm never going to be the center of my mother's attention."

With the men in her life, Dee tried to replay her attempts at being the center of attention, and ended up always *giving*—gifts, time, errands, favors. She picked men who never gave her what she needed, replaying the situation with her mother's inattention.

With men, Dee played her "ideal" of mother-role, giving them what she had wanted to receive from her mother. But somehow she always had the gnawing sensation that she didn't have the right to someone's company or love or attention and that she had to buy it.

In a dialogue with her Inner Therapist, Dee talked about this feeling of having to buy love from her latest boyfriend.

INNER THERAPIST: Dee, remember all the times before. Remember how you said he calls only when he needs something. You don't have to be bothered by this. You can put an end to it by not accepting his calls. For your own good, don't accept the call.
DEE: But he'll get mad. If he gets mad I won't hear from him again. If I don't hear from him again, I'll get lonely.

INNER THERAPIST: What are you getting from him anyway?

DEE: I'm getting some attention from him.

INNER THERAPIST: But the grief, pain, and feelings of unworthiness far outweigh the immediate gratification from the attention. Your life is not going to end—you'll still live if you don't get attention from him. I know you thought you couldn't survive without him, or without any of the others that went before him.

DEE: You're right. My life would go on. I'll survive. He's not the most important thing in the world. And I'm not the most important thing in his world. There are other people. And there will be other people that care about me.

Thereafter Dee began to pay more attention to the voice of her Inner Therapist, and her attempts to get attention from her mother and boyfriend began to lessen. Paradoxically, an immediate fringe benefit was that her boyfriend began, for the first time, to give her some unsolicited attention.

Another young woman, Lola, replayed submerged aspects of life with mother. She selected men who were weak, fed them until they were strong, then left them before they rejected her. With the help of her Inner Therapist she was able to confront this recurrent theme and free herself from the necessity of repeating it.

Awareness of how dominant a role the primary parent plays in our lives is essential if we are to loosen the repetitive patterns that chain us, often so destructively, to our past.

Not only do mothers have a profound effect on our lives, but we may in turn affect theirs. Natalia, a middle-aged grandmother, held her mother's death in her hands and had to face an awesome decision—to kill or not to kill.

One Saturday night I received a call from Natalia. She said her mother, aged ninety-three, was dying. Natalia was crying, not because of her mother's imminent death, which she had anticipated for a long time and felt resigned to, but because of her own suffering. The story came out between sobs—her mother, Paula, had severe osteoporosis and advanced arteriosclerosis. She had lived in a nursing home for the past five years and Natalia had dutifully and lovingly visited her regularly.

Three days ago, Paula suddenly developed a massive cerebral infarct—that is, the blood supply to a large section of her brain was cut off and she slipped into a coma. The doctor gave Natalia these options:

1. He could operate immediately, in which case Paula would probably die on the operating table, he said, because of her frail condition.

2. He could start all kinds of life-support systems—tubes, iv's, catheters, etc., in which case she could linger on, comatose but alive, for an indeterminate period of time.

3. He could do nothing except give her morphine for her pain, and nothing else and let nature take its course. The nurses had already tried to feed Paula by mouth—a tablespoon of warm milk, which she had aspirated into her lungs.

All along, since she had entered the nursing home, Paula had made Natalia promise that she wouldn't let her die in a hospital, that she would take her home to die. Natalia had agreed, and now told the doctor she wanted to take her mother home. Paula had also told Natalia she didn't want to have a lingering death.

The choice was predetermined—Natalia would take Paula home. The doctor gave Natalia a large supply of morphine, with instructions on how to give the shots to Paula whenever she was in pain or too restless.

For three days Natalia cared for Paula with the assistance of round-the-clock nurses. One of the nurses, who worked a shift at the upstate New York nursing home and had known Paula for the past several years, was very fond of her and wanted to be with her to give her solace and to ease her dying.

And now here was Natalia, crying on the phone with me, three days after bringing Paula home to die. I was wondering why Natalia was calling me—was it for solace and comfort, or what? Suddenly Natalia blurted out the reason for her call: "I can't stand to see her like this. She's suffering so much, but she won't let go. I can't bear it. Her feet are turning black, and it's going up her ankles. I could end her agony if I gave her a large dose of morphine. The reason I'm in a hurry and am calling you on a Saturday night is that the nurse will be leaving in a couple of hours and she said she'd want me to do it on her shift so there would be no repercussions afterward. She's trustworthy and she loves my mother."

"Then you've decided to kill your mother?" I asked.

"Yes, we all think it would be the best."

I remained silent for a while, absorbing what Natalia had just told me.

103

NATALIA: What are you thinking? Usually you come right out and tell me. Is there something wrong?

EILEEN: I'm still absorbing what you said. Apparently you're ambivalent about the right or wrong of the act of killing your mother, or you would have done it straightaway and not called me about it. What do the others say?

NATALIA: Richard and the children are all for it. They see how much suffering there is.

EILEEN: And you've called me for permission?

NATALIA: I just wanted to be sure I wasn't overlooking something.

EILEEN: Well, you say your mother had told you not to let her linger with dying. That's what she *said*. But you are also telling me she's hanging on to life with every shred possible. Her *behavior* belies her words. She's acting as though she doesn't want to let go, you say, and yet you're planning to make her die right now. Look, I can't answer the question for you. But there inside of you is your own therapeutic principle, a force in you that is interested first in your own survival. That force is your Inner Therapist. She is not interested in your highs or lows, your good or bad feelings. She is interested only in your survival and in the survival of your species. Put that Inner Therapist in front of you and ask her the question you've asked me. Listen to what she tells you.

(There is a long pause.)

EILEEN: What is your Inner Therapist saying?

NATALIA (*as her* INNER THERAPIST): Paula would be better off if you did it.

EILEEN: Wait a minute. *Who* would be better off?

NATALIA: Paula. We'd all be relieved if she died now instead of continuing to suffer.

EILEEN: That sounds like *your* reasoning. Your Inner Therapist isn't concerned with such things as who's happier or better off. She's concerned with your *survival needs*. So ask her again. Don't *tell* her *your* answer—ask her for hers. Ask her straight whether you should kill Paula now.

NATALIA (*pause, then softly, hesitantly):* Should I kill Paula now?

EILEEN: Now be your Inner Therapist. What is she saying?

NATALIA (*long pause, as though tuning in):* She says, "I don't know if you could stand the guilt afterward."

EILEEN: Natalia, this is the first time you've mentioned guilt. Before, you made it seem as though there was no contest, that you had no ambivalence about killing Paula with morphine. It was all set, and simple, and everyone, including the nurse, was for it. Now your Inner Therapist has brought up a new thing— guilt. I'd like to hear more from her. Let her talk directly to you. Put her in front of you and let her address you and talk directly to you.

INNER THERAPIST: Natalia, I don't know if you can stand the guilt. You may not be able to afterward.

EILEEN: Now answer her.

NATALIA: I think I can. I have Paula's strength in me.

EILEEN: And what does your Inner Therapist say to that?

INNER THERAPIST: You do have Paula's strength, but the guilt of killing her may be too much for you to bear—

NATALIA (interrupting): I didn't think of that at all before. I think she's right. But I can't bear to see Paula like this. I can't bear to see that black color going up into her legs.

EILEEN: Yes, it's probably gangrene. But you know she can't go on much longer like this. Nature will take its course.

NATALIA: I can't stand it. She might go on for days and days.

EILEEN: She's had no food or water for three days. She can't last much longer. She's probably all dehydrated. It seems you won't have to kill her. Nature is taking care of that.

NATALIA: Yes. I guess it was my own suffering I was thinking of. I didn't think *I* could stand it any longer.

EILEEN: Even in her comatose state, Paula has made the decision to hang on to her last thread. In deciding to let *her* decide, you have given her responsibility for her own life and death and not taken this away from her. At the same time, you have relieved yourself once and for all of the necessity of carrying whatever recriminations of guilt might later have come up as a result of your killing your mother.

Natalia was relieved to have made this decision. The relief gave her a spurt of forcefulness which she would use to face the ordeal of watching her comatose mother slowly die.

As she was expressing her relief and her renewed fortitude she was called urgently away. "They're calling me—I have to go. I'll talk to you later."

One hour later Natalia called me back. Her mother had died. I was relieved that Natalia had decided not to kill her mother, had not hastened Paula's end in order to end her own suffering.

And it was Natalia's own Inner Therapist who had given her the key by reminding her of the inevitable guilt that must come from matricide, even matricide of a comatose, brain-ravaged, vegetative ninety-three-year-old mother.

Commonly we blame the failure of a love relationship on the partner, the "other," blithely forgetting that it takes two to tango. To complicate things further, each person drags her or his past into the relationship—especially the earliest and most influential members of that past.

However, although most people are prone to blame the "other," there are some, men and women alike, who feel so worthless and undesirable that they take the entire blame on their own shoulders.

Both extremes are shortsighted. And each extreme avoids dealing with the opposite pole. That is, blamers fail to see the role they themselves play, *and why,* in damaging the relationship. Self-deprecators refuse to face the contributions for failure by the other, taking all the blame upon themselves.

If you are at one pole or the other, there is much you can gain by exploring the opposite, hidden pole within yourself.

For example, Glenn felt like a whipped cur every time his wife berated him. Usually feeling insignificant, he was bathed in appreciativeness by the mere fact of his wife's putting up with him. In his business affairs, he had the same demeanor, feeling like the lowest and most worthless scum at business meetings. He never looked at anyone during those meetings, keeping his gaze fixed on his portfolio.

As a boy, Glenn was treated like an invalid. His father told him it was dangerous for him to play football, and he was supposed to come home directly from school every day. Glenn managed to play ball surreptitiously, however, but he always felt terribly guilty. At home, his father, a hypochondriac, dominated his every move and was oversolicitous about every breath Glenn took. He made Glenn go to bed hours earlier than necessary, and Glenn would lie awake for hours.

When Glenn began to explore the pole of the blamer he came in contact with a whining, complaining, worrying quality that reminded him most disagreeably of his father. Blaming, for Glenn, together with any aggressive or dominating behavior, evoked the father who

106

had robbed him of a carefree childhood and from whom Glenn had earlier withdrawn.

It wasn't until Glenn stopped his concealment and confronted that whining bully of a father ensconced within himself that he began to graduate from the status of a whipped dog and assume the upright position of a man. Afterward, his relationship with his wife improved remarkably. And at business meetings be began to use his eyes to connect with the other eyes around him.

Glenn is yet another example of how difficult it is to have a fulfilling adult relationship with others until the relationship with the self and what that self harbors are confronted and fulfilled.

Knowledge of the *self* includes, of course, not only the psychological self but the physical self as well. Perhaps it might be said that the prerequisite of knowing another body well is to know one's own body fully. You'd be astonished at how *little* people know of their bodies, especially women.

Thelma, a mother of five children, was a college graduate with a doctoral degree in chemistry. She was a bright, well-read, intelligent woman. I recall how shocked she was when, while discussing childbirth and related matters with me, I mentioned there was a urethral opening for excreting urine as well as a vaginal opening for sexual and procreative functions and for menstrual excretions. She was absolutely stunned at her own ignorance, for in other areas she had such an open, inquisitive mind.

Men too are subject to repressive forces, especially macho men who have to keep making conquests and dominating women in order to prove *to themselves* that they are virile. The exaggerated "potency" they display is a thin veneer covering their self-doubts, their lack of self-acceptance.

The bigger the macho obsession looms on their outside, the smaller and more fearful they feel on the inside. That is, the more "meek-feminine" they feel internally, the more "bravado-masculine" they have to act on the outside to maintain the disguise.

The macho doth protest too much, methinks.

The look at yourself, physical and psychological and emotional, aided by your Inner Therapist, can help you in one of the most vital relationships given you by life—the relationship with your child. Jennifer, a thirty-year-old married woman with a ten-year-old son, Calvin, came to see me in a consultation because she beat him mercilessly and feared she might kill him in one of her rages. With great difficulty she confessed her recurrent flare-ups with Calvin

107

and her hatred of him. She felt very guilty, and her confession came out haltingly.

During the session, I introduced Jennifer to her Inner Therapist and suggested that Jennifer talk with *her,* for *she* could help her much more than could I.

Jennifer looked at me as though I was daft and offered a lot of resistance but finally relented. With considerable reluctance she began to get into the role of the Inner Therapist, and she gradually stopped the haltingness of her speech. What most impressed her in the dialogue was that her Inner Therapist *did not sit in judgment* of her. It was an utterly new experience. In that conversation what emerged, in addition to her hatred and abuse of Calvin, was her resentment of how her mother used to push her and her father around, and how she hated that, and hated her father for not standing up to her mother.

Jennifer's Inner Therapist described Jennifer's brutality toward Calvin in a way that awakened Jennifer's sympathy for her son, a sympathy she had never before felt.

About a month later I heard from Jennifer. She marveled at how the dialogue with her Inner Therapist had changed her relationship with Calvin. "It's so different, it feels like a miracle," she said. Her abusive behavior had changed, although it seemed to Jennifer that Calvin himself had changed: "Somehow he's different toward me. He comes over spontaneously to hug me—something he hasn't done for years!"

I present Jennifer's experience with her Inner Therapist not to raise your expectations of miracles but to encourage you to question the "uncontrollable" behaviors and feelings which you suppose dominate your relationships and which you may erroneously suppose you are wedded to forever.

Change can come about with great and diligent labor. It may, sometimes, come as easily and effortlessly as a light fall of rain, or a teardrop.

Finally, any discussion of sexual relations in our era of bigger-is-better and more-is-better-yet, especially as it relates to orgasm, would be incomplete without some counterpoint to the trend of "once is not enough."

With so much focus—amounting almost to an obsessive frenzy—on conforming to *quantity,* sheer numbers become the end-all. What is often lost is the *sensation,* the quality of the feelings and the quality of the relationship.

In the sexual encounter, the quality of the contact of two loving partners, the heat and excitement flowing to and from each other, the arousal of the yearnings for caress and touch and holding, the heart's opening up to the flow of tenderness and caring—all of this and so much more is frequently lost in the slam-bam-thank-you-ma'am rush to "achieve orgasm." All that heat turns into one big, anxious Achievement Test.

To the extent that the upcoming orgasm gets prime attention and concern—the yes or no of it, the now or later of it—to that extent the partners are *outside* the experience and living for later: the *later* of the anxiously awaited single or multiple orgasm—and not for the *now* of the sensual nurturance.

How many potentially beautiful shared hours have you lost, as have untold otherwise-loving couples, by the anxious focus on orgasm as a goal instead of on the sensation of contact in the *now* of the sexual embrace?

Cupid waits with his bow and arrows to penetrate your heart so that it will flow out to others and allow their hearts to flow into yours. Your Inner Therapist waits, too, to guide you to Cupid's waiting place.

9
Inner Therapist Workshop

The strongest thing is necessity, for it masters all.
—Thales, in Diogenes Laërtius,
Lives and Opinions of Eminent Philosophers

There go my people. I must follow them, for I am their leader.
—Mahatma Gandhi

I'm not okay, you're not okay, and that's okay
—Leon Lurie, psychoanalyst, Washington, D.C.,
in a personal communication

You probably have heard of the Rorschach test, those inkblots onto which you project some of your deepest psychological secrets, a study of which is supposed to help reveal who you really are inside your masks but too often only helps others study and diagnose those masks which are evident anyway.

It is also evident that our bodies are capable of revealing even our most shamefully guarded secrets. Indeed, we are walking Rorschachs!

Recall Millicent's running nose and how it revealed her running from the fear of her father's insane behavior—and perhaps her own? And Mike-the-convict's asymmetrical mouth and his fear of being on the level; Steve's ulcerous belly and his hidden rage; and so on.

Another person not mentioned earlier is Corinne, a young woman with a uterine fibroid. When Corinne gave her fibroid a voice and "permitted" it to describe itself, it said: "I am tough, fibrous, resistant. I don't shrink away. I stay put. I take up space, and I cause pain and trouble."

Corinne was a meek, shrinking violet, scared to death of her own shadow (but more scared of her power and strength—qualities she kept in dark interior recesses). She withdrew from hurting others, preferring to be hurt herself—an absorber of other people's pain.

111

As Corinne shrank on the outside, the tough fibroid kept growing on the inside. Corinne needed to hear the words of that tough uterine growth and use them as a guide to her internal force.

For those of you who are wallflowers of whatever variety or gender (including the numerous shrinking violets among the male population), the following exercises might prove helpful:

1. List, with the help of your Inner Therapist, all the people who flatten you out, push you against the wall, frighten or startle or threaten you in any way.
2. Describe in detail
   a. *How* they do it:
      suddenly argue and criticize
      never look at you or seem to recognize you
      treat you as insignificant, lowly . . . etc.
   b. What they *look* like when they're doing it:
      frown
      set jaw
      red in the face
      down-curved mouth . . . etc.
   c. What they are *doing* when they do it:
      yelling
      throwing things
      speaking through clenched teeth . . . etc.
   d. What they are *saying* or sounding like:
      "Why don't you . . .!"
      "Listen here now . . .!" etc.
   e. What *they* seem to be feeling when they do it:
      hate
      fury
      disgust . . . etc.
3. Describe *your feelings* (fear, worry, etc.) in all their shades and nuances when those persons push you.
4. Use your creative imagination
   a. Picture the most threatening of the people in the list in 1.
   b. Picture the worst details of 2.
   c. Picture the feeling causing the greatest suffering in 3.

Do (a), (b), and (c) one at a time. Then mentally combine these in an exaggerated melodramatic scenario resulting in your literally being plastered against the wall, flattened out to a two-dimensional figure.

If you want to have a therapeutic experience, if you want to have it right now so that you don't have to run to a psychiatrist's office for it, it's available for you there, right where you are. *Instant therapy!*

Just stop reading forward at this point and go back to work out items 1 through 4.

Do the work slowly, carefully, seriously, grimly if you must, or even humorously, but make sure to do it thoroughly. It's an edifice to yourself you're building, and the foundation must be solid.

After you've done the suggested task, do it again, this time unleashing even more attacking details. Focus on that person or group of persons who make you shrink.

Enhance the image of your own whimpering fearfulness. Enlarge every detail until you become indistinguishable from the rest of the patterns on the wallpaper.

If you really want to get going with your imaginativeness, after you've been flattened out you might picture your assaulters still going strong, continuing to pick at you, until you lose another dimension and become a mere dot, or even a dim remnant of one. Or until you disappear altogether into no dimension at all.

Yes, go extreme. Carry your shrinking-violet state to its ultimate extremity—dissolution. Let yourself feel that dissolution, that disappearance, that being *invisible*. It's the ultimate achievement, the goal that you have distorted and contorted your life to achieve. So that all those shrinking distortions shall not have been made in vain, carry it out to an extreme and feel that ultimate state.

The important lesson here is that people usually stop short of carrying out their ultimate design. Thus they relinquish their power by having to carry out, over and over again, the intermediate states, pulling back time and again from the goal and thus never resolving anything. To regain your force, carry out to its extreme in your imagination your present state—whether it is a condition of wallflowerness, isolation, promiscuity, lovelessness, or whatever. In carrying this out to its excruciating extreme in your mind, you give yourself a chance to *discover* the underlying purpose your state or condition serves. Once you accept *your purpose,* you can release the energy you've spent concealing that purpose from yourself and thus have the energy available to you for more constructive uses.

Feel what it's like finally to be not shrinking but shrunk, shrunk to nondimensionality. Feel what it's like to be *invisible*.

Achieve the ultimate goal of all your withdrawingness, shyness, pullings away. What is it like to be untouchable, unseeable, impalpable to feeling and to sight, like Macbeth's imaginary dagger?

Feel the *power* in that. No one can get you. No one can get at you anymore. You are free. Feel the freedom in that. No dimension makes you omni-dimensional. You, a timid violet, have become inviolable. *Feel it.* Revel in it. Luxuriate in it.

You are finally everywhere and nowhere. Ahh, at last. Free, powerful, unassailable. *You never knew you had it in you*—that power. That wonderful ultimate absence that makes you universally present.

Give yourself several minutes of wandering, floating, flowing through the harshest of your assailants unencumbered, unhampered, so *fully you* that you are not and yet you *are.*

Open your mind to your total dimensionality by having no dimensions at all.

Your assaulters have helped bring you to this state.

Let us now, as we must in all affairs that treat the human condition, balance our vision and look at the *opposing* view which is also part of our condition, although we would love to think of it as coming from *out there.*

To suggest where I am heading, I'd like to digress momentarily. (Did you expect *anything* in life or good therapeutic encounters to go in a *straight,* uninterrupted line? Growth takes place unevenly, oddly.)

A psychotherapist friend was asked to lead a workshop on the nuclear threat to the world. She told me she had run into a snag in planning it because "people are already very worried about it and I don't want to create any more anxiety."

"Oh," I said, "how about dealing with the nuclear explosiveness within each participant? Isn't the reason we don't do more *out there,* the reason we protect the nuclear hawks with our passivity—isn't the reason for our shrinking from effectively doing anything about it that we have not dealt with those very factors inside our selves, our own atomic explosiveness hidden within?"

"Yes!" She smiled. "That's right. I hadn't gone far enough to look at it that way. Thanks. I can get the ball rolling now." And she went on to give a dynamic and significant workshop.

So now, back to you, and the other character in your shrinking-violet drama. The flip side of your timid shrinking-violet self is the combination of the would-be mockers, disdainers, deprecators, out-

and-out attackers. Those whose acceptance you crave and whose judgment you fear will always find you wanting.

It doesn't have to be significant people in your life—although it usually is, at least initially, before the condition spreads. It can be anyone at all—a stranger sitting next to you in an airplane, the people at a party, those at your work. They don't even have to be big-deal people for you to shrink from them. Even people you'll never see after this moment can be used to perpetrate your drama of a shy, shrinking flower.

If you've taken your shrinking-violet status seriously in your life, you may have had trouble when I suggested that you visualize someone flattening you out. If that sounded too farfetched for you to imagine, it only shows how powerful you've been in taming your would-be assailants—a typical martyr power, the power of the weak and vulnerable.

So if people have always treated you with kid gloves, delicately as with an invalid, and your ploy works well to keep would-be flatteners at bay, then you'll have to give a wilder swing to your imagination when you picture your antagonist, or go farther back in your life, away from the present, and imagine who is the Central Identified Antagonist there. Whoever that may be—from your past, your present, or your imagined future, or from all three time zones at once—focus in on the frightening characteristics of that person. And go through the procedure from the vantage point of the Antagonist.

Build on air, if you must, on nuance, on innuendo, and once you have a thread to go on, build on that. Keep building, constructing the image, until your Antagonist takes form, sturdy enough to threaten you. Then build on that.

If your life has been severely sheltered, if you've lived as in a hothouse with no inclement winds to blow against you, build the Antagonist from fables—the big bad wolf, the evil stepmother, the wicked witch. There is incorporated somewhere inside you a model of the Antagonist to build from. Build it from the blueprint in your *inner* dimensions, those which have been so *inner* that they have eluded your own vision.

You are now about to improve your visual acuity, so go to it. Build the image—the craftiest, most judgmental, most deprecatory Central Identified Antagonist you can possibly imagine, crushing you to the wall by word or deed, by physical force, by a look, by lording it over you or by ignoring you. Anything, everything that evokes in

115

you the feeling of being insignificant, squashed.

We are here not focusing on your victim feelings but on the Antagonist's brute force over you. Keep the focus there—all your attention on the Antagonist. Get to recognize that person, those factors, those groups. In whatever way it (or they) exclude you or contribute to your sitting against the wall at the dance of life, visualize it, extend it, join forces with it, and increase its power.

Focus so much on the Antagonist that you leave the wall and *become that excluder*, that antagonist, that would-be assailant. Feel its contempt in a sneer of your own. That is, feel your own sneer on your face. Become the sneerer, the denigrator. Go on. No one is watching, not even the shrinking violet who observes only his or her own shrinking.

Feel the presence of that Central Identified and Powerful Antagonist—it'd be a quantum leap should you do this. For the law of opposites dictates that every extreme state, psychological or emotional, balances an opposing internal condition.

And the most effective way of dealing with these external extremes is to uncover and contact the internal ones.

But because this inside condition is the realm of the most intense secret, whose revelation is not only forbidden but steeped in the deepest pain, most people willingly hold on to the external state—no matter its crosses to bear, its slings and arrows to suffer. For nothing is as scathing, as immolating, as that internal secreted entity. And nothing can be as curative, liberating, humanizing.

Most of us live one- or at best two-dimensional lives because the intense interior third-dimension is too hot to handle. It takes the best therapist in the world to help us handle this. This is our own Inner Therapist, available to help us reveal the secrets we have kept from ourselves, to help us read our body's inkblots, sun spots, stains, and other imperfections, to help us contact our shameful realities hiding within and bring them out to the light of our minds and so diminish our need for the covering shadows, the cover-ups.

We create external psychological and emotional distortions as camouflages, fig leaves, to cover up our naked and shameful humanity. We need to let our Inner Therapist lead us back to the Garden, where we can reclaim our naked, uncertain, ambivalent and simple humanness.

And now, *welcome to the Inner Therapist Workshop.*
There is no "leader" here, outside of your *self*.

Our goal is to find ways and means to contact your Inner Therapist through her or his various voices and to hear the message meant for your ears alone, the message designed by Nature herself to guide your growth toward your own wholeness, completeness, and maturity.

The questions that I will be suggesting in some of the following exercises are not intended to be ends in themselves. If you lend yourself to this process, these questions and the answers they evoke will probably lead you to other questions of your own making and still other answers. This is how the creative mind works—leaping along from one stepping-stone to another, sometimes across a rivulet, sometimes stuck in the mud, almost never in a straight and easy line, and rarely if ever *predictable*.

So make sure to note those questions and the diverse answers your mind leads you to . . . in whatever digressive direction they seem to be taking you.

Have a productive journey!

STEP 1

And now, to begin. Have with you a notebook and a pen, a box of tissues in case of need, and, if you like, a tape recorder to help you record the event and concretize the experience.

STEP 2

Find a room where you can be alone and where you can make some noise if necessary without someone calling the paddy wagon or interrupting you. If noise is a problem—that is, *your* noise—have with you a pillow in the event you might want to give some unencumbered yells. As you speak in different tongues, you'll want to be sure to protect all of your voices from external interference.

STEP 3

Before you start doing the following assignments, take several full, deep breaths. This will enhance your circulation, relax you for the anticipated tasks, and help you have better contact with your body. If you breathe too fast, as in a galloping rhythm—hyperventilating—you'll probably get anxious. There's already enough anxiety waiting within, so slow the breathing down to an amble. Concentrate on your breathing. Take deep abdominal breaths, exhaling *fully*.

117

Make sure you're in a comfortable position. Make sure also that you avoid any stimulants or drugs of any sort before, during, and after these exercises—including caffeine (coffee or tea), nicotine, alcohol, tranquilizers, etc. There will be more than enough other obstacles to overcome, and you're better off contacting your Inner Therapist in a drug-free state.

Now you are ready for some physical assessments.

Step 4 A

Check out how you are sitting. Let your mind scan your body. Assess how your head is held, what your arms are doing, your legs, your back, your neck and shoulders, your stomach, your eyes. Do this at random, with no particular order. If you allow this, you will come on to a body part and how it is positioned—limp, rigid, loose—as a *discovery*. Your mind will lead you to the part that calls for your attention if you let it flow without directings. Stop reading now and just concentrate on your body.

Don't try to correct anything your mind lights on. Neither unfurrow your forehead nor uncross your legs. Take them as they are, for as they are and as you are at this very moment gives you an opportunity to tune in to the channel through which you may hear your Inner Therapist.

Recall, your Inner Therapist speaks to you through your asymmetries, your imperfections, your tensions, your pains. Your job is to learn what is being said to you. What must you understand about your *self* in order to grow into that self, in order to reach toward wholeness?

Once you have gone this far and settled upon a body part, you are ready to use your notebook and pen. Write an objective description of that part on which your mind has lighted. Be as accurate and detailed as possible. Leave no angle out. In your mind's eye or in a looking glass, or both, study that part. Describe what it *looks like,* much as a camera would. If it's something like a balding head under your toupee, or sagging breasts under your Maidenform, or triple chins under your turtleneck, you may have trouble describing these parts as a lens would—detailed and without derision. But if you begin to lose your objectivity and start to pour contempt on the part, you will cloud your vision and won't be able to see what's right in front of your eyes. (Much as reading a critic's review before you see a play can cloud your own vision in the theatre, even from third row center.)

118

So—criticism, judgment, contempt are out of order at this time. We are interested here in *objective measurements,* without feelings or judgments, heartless, mindless.

This is easy for me to say and difficult for you to do, for the part that has the most to say to you is probably the very same part you have tried so hard to squelch. Therefore, you will have to pay strict attention here. Anything that a cold objective lens would not see must be avoided.

Later you may rage, rage against the part, or cover it over with your concealing devices. Now you are to invite that part out to be weighed and measured, promising it in advance that it won't have to suffer your scorn. You must not betray that trust.

Since this is not your customary response—this objectivity—you will undoubtedly have trouble with this assignment. If so, do not move on to the next step. Stop here and repeat it. Continue to repeat your attempts to describe with a cold eye what you see. You are not being asked to *love* the part, only to measure it without judging its dimensions or characteristics.

Do this over and over until, perhaps, you become so bored with it that the heat of your contempt cools and you begin to look at the part in its naked state without prejudice.

On the other hand, some of you may live quite well with your body, acceptantly. In your case you may have no trouble with the contempt I've anticipated. Your mind might have been drawn simply to a particular position—let's say, crossed legs. Fine. Without changing your position, describe those legs, what they are doing, which one is on top, what the position itself results in, what portion of the legs cross, which does not, etc.

This step is not to be an analysis of whys and wherefores. It's merely a description of what *is.* Now, if you have carried out the foregoing in as objective a manner as possible, you are ready for the next part of Step 4.

Step 4 B

What does the chosen part feel like right now? Is it numb, tingly, bloated, shrunken, pained, tight, loose, rigid, soft, stuffed, starved, cool, warm—or what?

You are not to intrude your feelings *about the part.* (Ah-ha!—see how quickly you revert to judgment and contempt?)

The feelings *in the part* are what we're after, not your attitudes or reactions to it.

With your mind focused on the part, write down the feelings in that part. Again, keep in mind the metaphor of the lens that has no judgment. Having survived Step 4 A, you should be able to complete Step 4 B readily.

Step 4 C

Now you are ready to reap the rewards of your labor. Setting aside the body part that provoked the description in Steps 4 A and 4 B, read the descriptions you have written out of their original context. Instead of "it," use the personal pronoun "I."

For example, from Chapter 1 you may recall that the hunching shoulders said, "I am hunched up . . ." Now, if you were to take this statement out of the shoulder context and personalize it, say it as your *self*, then the phrase "I am hunched up" takes on a new meaning, more global, a statement to you about your *life*.

Listen to the new meaning you get when you personalize those descriptions about your body parts. Let the new meaning lead to other global statements, other meanings. Similarly, in Step 4 B, a statement about the feelings in the body part, heard as a statement about your life, may become an illumination of that life.

For example, "I feel tight" may bring all sorts of meanings to you: I am ungenerous, stingy, I am constipated in my feelings, I am closed off, and so on. Wherever the associations lead you, follow, even if it makes you wince. The wince is evidence that you've tuned in to the right channel. Therefore it should be most welcomed. Now you are ready to proceed.

Step 4 D

The question "What function does it serve?" is helpful in a great many situations. It is a potentially enlightening query.

For example, passive, submissive parents, fearful of saying the least boo, are often shocked to learn that the wild outbursts of their behavior-disordered kids serve the function of expressing some of their own aggression that has been buried within themselves. But it was not so deeply buried that it didn't in some way get communicated to their kids, who then had to shoulder the responsibility and the consequences of that rebellious behavior which their parents dared not own up to.

Ask yourself the following questions:

1. What functions do the characteristics uncovered in Step 4 A serve?

2. What functions do the feelings in Step 4 B serve?

120

3. What functions are served by characteristics and feelings uncovered in Step 4 C?

4. How do these characteristics and feelings help me?

5. How do these hinder me?

Now put your Inner Therapist before you. Ask her or him those questions, one at a time, giving space and time for your Inner Therapist to answer you. By now, with your exercises in objectivity, you have taken some steps to derail your own habitual prejudgments and automatic responses. You are ready to receive help from your Inner Therapist in understanding the *functional purpose* of your body's positions, imperfections, blemishes, sensations. You are ready to receive insights—sightings within—from your internal guide to your life force. Have your Inner Therapist address you by your name, and then go on to answer your questions.

Write down every word as it emerges from your Inner Therapist, no matter how distasteful, fanciful, outrageous, fearful. Remember, your Inner Therapist is *not* interested in your happy-hour highs or your Monday-morning blues, only in your survival needs and those of your species. If you start coming out with words satisfying your *wants,* you will know that these come from the you trained to have certain culturally determined wants and not from your Inner Therapist, whose orders come only from pervasive Mother Nature herself, looking to keep her charges alive and growing. ("I *need* a cigarette" is a common misnomer for a *want.*)

When you have finished writing the words emerging from your Inner Therapist, enter into a dialogue with her or him. If you are open to this process, more questions will inevitably arise. Write these down. Then write your reactions to what your Inner Therapist has said. Continue the dialogue until nothing more emerges. Be certain, if you have some *feeling* flowing, that you describe this feeling in writing too. This writing, this dialogue, with your Inner Therapist will aid your journey into your *self.*

Step 5 A

This step is intended particularly for those of you who have disturbing *symptoms,* whether in the emotional realm (such as depressions, fears, anxieties, rages), the somatic or physical realm (headaches, bellyaches, constipation, allergies), the psychological realm (suspiciousness, phobias, obsessions, addictions), or the sexual and relationship realm (sexual turmoil or dysfunction, jealousies, alienation, isolation).

121

As was stated earlier, it goes against the grain to consider the symptom as other than a blight to be gotten rid of. Here, in this exercise, you are being asked to suspend that belief and look at the symptom as an opportunity to learn that thing about your *self* of which you are in dire need.

You are asked to consider the symptom as a *creation* of your life force, forged as a necessity to keep you in balance, to help you grow toward your potential. You are being asked to consider that *cutting off the symptom because it disturbs is like cutting out your heart because it aches.*

The aching heart and the disturbing symptom certainly need attending to. Pain is there for your protection. Here, in this exercise, you are to learn to be protective toward your own creation, your own symptom, disturbing and distressing though it may be.

1. Following the example in Step 4, write an objective description of the symptom.

2. Take the role of the symptom and describe your functions.

For example, with depression you might say:

I am Isabel's depression.

I make her feel low, energyless, without desire to do anything, worthless, take no pleasure in anything, have no hope for change for the better.

I give her crying spells, make her lose interest in her husband, her children, her work . . . And on and on.

Or, with obesity:

I am Horace's fat body, two hundred pounds overweight.

I drag him down.

Everyone looks at me when he walks by.

He has trouble fitting into seats in public places.

I am an endless source of embarrassment to him.

I threaten his health.

The bigger I am, the more attention people pay me. And the more I make Horace pay attention to me too . . . And on and on.

STEP 5 B

After writing the description of the symptom in its many aspects, follow the lead of that description and devise a list of questions. For instance, with Isabel's depression, she might, upon reading her foregoing description (Step 5 A), come up with questions like the following:

Who makes (or made) me feel low?

Who takes (or took) away my energy?

Who takes (or took) away my desire or prevents me from doing anything?

Who makes (or made) me feel worthless?

Who prevents (or prevented) me from having pleasure?

Who makes (or made) me feel hopeless?

Who makes (or made) me cry?

Who prevents or takes away my interest in my husband? my children? my work?

The tendency for someone like Isabel would be to answer all the foregoing questions by blaming *herself*. That is, for the oppressed/depressed or masochistically oriented person the easiest answer to the questions is "myself," "I'm to blame." It is almost automatic. And the answer—*I* make myself feel worthless because I am worthless—perpetuates and reinforces the depressed condition. And so this tendency must be guarded against here.

Considerable effort is required to *discover* answers that are not ready-made or automatic. Are you prepared to go beyond your reflexes and learn, who, indeed, has made you sad, cry, feel worthless, etc?

And, if you are someone with Horace's condition, you might construct the following questions from the description given in Step 5 A:

Who drags (or dragged) me down?

Who is (or was) like a two-hundred-pound weight I have to carry?

Whom do I (did I) want to look at me when I walk by?

Who gives (or gave) me trouble fitting into seats in public places?

Who was (or is) an endless source of embarrassment to me?

Who threatens my health? Or, Who threatens me?

Whom do (or did) I want to pay attention to me?

What in myself do I need to pay attention to?

What do I need to pay attention to?

In constructing the questions from your own descriptive words, you need to allow your creative imagination to play somewhat with those descriptions until relevant questions emerge. You might study how this was done with Isabel's and Horace's descriptions as an aid in determining your own leading questions.

Sometimes it is very helpful to turn the descriptions upside down and catch the question by surprise. The "right" question often leads to an illumination, if not an epiphany. (Einstein tried to get simple answers to problems, but when he got a *simple question,* he said, then he heard God talking!)

An example of the topsy-turvy play would be if Horace, instead of asking, "Who threatens my health?" or "Who threatens me?" were to turn this around and ask. "Whom do I want to threaten?"

This upside-down affair is particularly relevant if you are a self-blaming type. In Isabel's case, for instance, she might have a breakthrough if she could ask, "Whom do I want to make cry?"

In both the above cases, it is important to note that the past tense is sometimes more fruitful than present diggings, since we carry the tyrannies of past relationships with us into our present and future unless somehow those past conflicts were resolved.

Step 5 C

Now that you have identified the persons who contributed to your plight, describe how they act or have acted at their tyrannous worst. Never mind that they are (were) also kind to you and that they love you. There have been many murderous deeds in human history committed in the name of love. And the most devastating actions against us are those done unwittingly and with good intentions, for against these we have no defense.

Describe those deeds against you and describe the perpetrators of those deeds in vivid detail. Was it a mother who forced you to finish your platter? Thus did Horace's mother, also threatening him that if he didn't finish his milk quickly enough she would put urine in it and make him drink it. Leave no detail out in following the nefarious ways those loving partners of your life, in whatever guise or role, cast their destructive barbs. Write up how they did it, what they said, what they looked like, and, finally, what you felt like— your despair—when they were doing their thing.

Take lots of time with this step. It is an important springboard to the next one.

Step 5 D

Now that you have identified and described the persons or factors that contributed to your plight, it is time to invoke the biblical eye-for-an-eye, even though you would shrink from such retaliatory action in real life. To encourage you to take this step, I'd like to remind you to consider that if you can't be free in your *mind,* in your creative imagination, where in the whole wide world *can* you be free?

And if you cannot own up to harboring evil impulses *within* you, you are doomed to contribute to the evil forces in others. Someone recently has said: *Evil is ordinary.* It seems to be awfully ordinary.

Remember, too, that this exercise is not being done to harm anyone—it is not being done in order for you to be against them. It is designed to be *for you.*

Nature demands that you be *for yourself,* and then *for others.* When you are not for yourself you pay a heavy penalty.

Your various symptoms are the cries of a body pitted against the self, the self betraying and tyrannizing that body and leaving it to express its despair and outrage in the only way it knows—the creation of symptoms.

In this step, then, you are to picture doing unto others the disturbing, destructive things they have done to you.

After you have managed to do this in your imagination, write a description of the events, no holds barred. Let your imagination run wild. It may be the only time in your life you ever gave yourself permission to do this.

Note that this is not a license to violent action but an invitation to release into your consciousness what has been slumbering all along in the dark recesses and shadows of your mind. You are not creating any new violence—you are merely liberating the violent retaliatory fantasies already there in order to liberate yourself from being the recipient of others' violations of you and from subtly contributing to those violations.

STEP 6

This is yet another helpful step. Place before you your objective guide, your Inner Therapist, and ask for help in answering the following questions:

1. What did I never say to my mother?
2. What did I never say to my father?
3. What did my mother never say to me?
4. What did my father never say to me?

Answer each question as fully and in as much detail as possible.

When you have exhausted the search for answers, begin to substitute other persons in place of your parents: grandparents, spouse, child, friend, neighbor, boss, employee, partner.

If you do this carefully, freeing your mind to *lead you,* you'll find a host of unspoken communications lying not far beneath the surface waiting to greet your mind and complete some old unfinished—and perhaps poignant—business.

STEP 7

Whatever the variety of symptoms that plague you, continue to search for the function or meaning as previously described. Continue your explorations via devising, creating, discovering appropriate questions.

For instance, with insomnia:

1. With the help of your Inner Therapist describe your tossings and turnings, your sleepless nights, your too-early awakenings, your inability to fall asleep, your consequent chronic fatigue.

2. Now your Inner Therapist will help you devise some questions that may run something like the following:

What happens when I stay awake at night?

What function does it serve?

What need do I have to stay awake? What is achieved by not sleeping?

A middle-aged father of three grown children, two of whom continued to live with him, discovered that the middle of the night was the only time he had to himself when he could read or think without being invaded.

In another instance, that of a premature birth, the mother might ask herself, after describing the delivery of a newborn one or two months early:

What function or need is served by my earlier delivery? What does my early delivery tell me that I need to hear?

A study of premature births conducted at Mt. Sinai Hospital in New York City several years ago indicated that the mothers in testing and interviews had a very high incidence of not wanting those babies for a variety of reasons, although *consciously* the mothers had been unaware of these attitudes. The findings contrasted sharply with those mothers carrying their babies to term.

STEP 8

Whatever the symptom, you may approach it in the manner indicated. Another sample approach follows:

I. Describe the symptom:
   What does it do?
   What does it feel like?
   What does it look like?
II. What are the *results* of having this symptom?
   Specifically, what does the symptom accomplish?
   What effect does it have on me?
   What effect does it have on others?
   List those others, and the symptom's variable effect on
   each one.
III. What subtle, underlying function does the symptom serve?
   What does it help me achieve?
   What does it hinder me from?
IV. What does the symptom teach me about my life? about my
   relationships?
V. What in my life and relationships needs airing, illumination,
   resolution? What is the connection between my symptom
   and those items?

You may notice that asking a similar question in a different way,
with a slightly different slant, may lead to an open sesame.

STEP 9

If, instead of a somatic or physical symptom you have an emotional one—let's say hatred of blacks, whites, Jews, Catholics, commu-
nists, Republicans, long-hairs, atheists, homosexuals, hawks,
doves—you'll know it's a disturbance by the very *excess* of your
feelings and reactions.

Generally, people suffering from prejudices, racisms, separatisms,
etc., do not see these states as symptoms of underlying disturbances,
especially if these symptoms synchronize with a generally accepted
view.

Sometimes an entire community or culture can suffer from mass
delusional symptoms with only a few dissenting exceptions here and
there.

The presence of the underlying disturbance can be contacted by
approaching these emotionalisms as you would any other symptom:

1. When did it begin? How did it start? What does it do? What
does it feel like?

2. What are the results? And so on.

Mostly, these attitudes are *not* subject to rational debate, for they
are emotionally based, and only emotions can cure emotions. It

takes a change of *feeling,* not facts, to change ideas that are fed from emotional sources.

This has not been an exhaustive Inner Therapist Workshop. It is, rather, an introductory course, indicating ways to approach the body's messages, be they in the form of physical, psychological or emotional symptoms. The messages are for your ears alone. Your messages come from your Inner Therapist, who is there to teach you about your needs, your necessities.

Our own voices tend generally to deal with our wants, which are usually the easy way out and often self-destructive.

The voice of your Inner Therapist is consistently relevant to your *needs,* needs for survival of the self and the species, needs for growth and for evolutionary development or change.

Mother Nature has done an unerring job in keeping the human species alive. She exists in every cell of our body and is there to guide our aliveness—not our happiness, joy, wealth, or party chattings of Michelangelo, but our sheer functional survival.

These nine steps of the Inner Therapist Workshop are presented here in the hope of providing you, the reader, with an introductory guide to contacting that oracle of survival which exists in each of you—your Inner Therapist.